Fire On Ice

Fire On Ice

ERIC LINDROS

WITH RANDY STARKMAN

HarperPaperbacks
A Division of HarperCollinsPublishers

HarperPaperbacks *A Division of* HarperCollins*Publishers*
10 East 53rd Street, New York, N.Y. 10022

First published by HarperCollinsPublishers Ltd in 1991. This updated edition published in 1992.

Cover photo by Claus Anderson
Cover design by Brant Cowie/ArtPlus Limited

First HarperPaperbacks printing: November 1992

Printed in the United States of America

HarperPaperbacks and colophon are trademarks of HarperCollins*Publishers*

10 9 8 7 6 5 4 3 2 1

Contents

Acknowledgments

A number of people were generous with their time and help in preparing this book. The authors would like to thank Pete Bell, Lisa Best, Bob Bishop, Gaye Black, Dave Branch, Sean Burke, Dan Cameron, Tony Cella, Rick Cornacchia, Mark Deazeley, John Futa, Curt Giles, Jeff Hardy, Dave Harlock, Matt Hoffman, Gil Hughes, Joe Juneau, Mike Keenan, Dave King, Dave LaFayette, Angelo Libertucci, Marg and Ed Lindros, Paul and Mary Lindros, Gabe Mancari, Jackie and Grant Marshall, Larry Marson, Roger Mepham, Marcia Miller, Frank Naylor, Doug Orr, Solomon Paquiz, Dawn and Ted Ralph, Ed Robicheau, Blake and Jean Roszell, Dan Roszell, Jim Rutherford, Brendan Shanahan, Brad Teichmann, Dick Todd, Mike Torchia, Bob, Lynn and Mark Vanderaa, Judy Vellucci, and Andy Wiedenbach.

The authors would also like to acknowledge Rick Curran and Gordon Kirke for their help in putting the book together, and publishers Stan and Nancy Colbert and Editor-in-Chief Iris Skeoch at HarperCollins for their guidance.

In addition, Randy Starkman would like to express his appreciation to Marg Lindros for the loan of her scrapbook, Moris Barmherzig for his generous advice, Asher Levy for his computer expertise and Michael Finewax and Denise Hynes for a hearty transcribing effort and other help. Most of all, Randy would like to thank his wife, Mary Hynes, for providing inspiration and support, not to mention her deft editing and writing touch.

To the Reader:

When we were first approached about doing a book, we almost immediately discarded the idea. When you write a book like this, you're opening up the front door of your house for people to come inside and walk through and look at things. We're a private family in many ways, so that aspect troubled us.

But as we thought about it more, we felt there could be some merits in the book, in that it would give people an opportunity to see Eric as an individual without the armor of a hockey player. We've also been very fortunate to have received sound advice from a lot of good people, and there are a few things we've learned as a family that we'd like to share.

Some people have asked: Why write a book now? Most books about athletes are written at the end of their careers. But although he's just starting professionally, Eric has been involved for many years in junior hockey and international hockey. The intention here isn't to write an autobiography. Instead, we wanted to deal with some of the things Eric experienced in his youth—a youth which is, unfortunately, coming to an end very quickly.

Eric has had an opportunity to enjoy a lot of things in hockey over the past few years. Perhaps this book will help some people to have that same thrill, to feel part of it.

So, our door is open. Welcome inside.

The Lindros Family

Fire On Ice

1

A Little Bit of Heaven

The clock is running down . . . barely time enough for one final rush against the league powerhouse.

They're decked out in black uniforms and we're wearing white. The contrast strikes me: the Good and the Evil. We're from Heaven, they're from Down Below. So far, it looks like Evil is ruling the day—but that's about to change.

We're racing in on a two-on-two. My winger goes wide. I fake going wide and cut inside, splitting the defense. I make a dash towards the net; the defensemen hack away at me on both sides, desperate to slow me down.

I shoot low for the corner on the left side. The goalie knows exactly where it's going and he lunges awkwardly for it—but too late.

The red light flashes. I raise my arms in celebration. And the crowd goes wild.

At least, it looked like the crowd was going wild. Even with my vivid imagination, it was a little hard to make out all those fans sitting there in the snowbank in the backyard of our home in London, Ontario. I had just returned home from our Saturday morning house league game and I was replaying the action on the backyard rink. It was a weekly ritual when I was a kid.

We got killed 11-1 in that game, but I couldn't wait to return to my rink to replay my goal all over again. I would think, "Where was everyone on the ice when I scored? How did the goalie react?" It was a great feeling to score in that game, because we were playing against the dominant team in the league. My best friends were on that team, and they whipped us every time we played them. Back on my rink, I would go through what everyone had done in the game—me and all the other seven-year-olds. I didn't repeat my mistakes, though. I would only replay things that were positive and that I enjoyed.

The rink was my getaway, my little bit of heaven. If I ever had a problem in school, I would get out on the rink and blow it off. Being on the rink was the best time of the day. You didn't care that your room needed cleaning, that you were supposed to help your brother with a project or anything like that. You just didn't obey. If my Mom, Bonnie, wanted to harp at me about something, she would have to climb through the snow to get to me. It was my escape from everything. When you were on the rink, it was like you were above the law.

My Mom was always buying us these funny-looking toques. They fit snugly over our heads so that our ears wouldn't freeze, and we could then put our helmets on top. We were always supposed to wear our helmets, because Bon the Nurse would flip out if we didn't. But if you were cagey enough, there were ways around that. When my Mom would be working away at the kitchen counter or going upstairs and couldn't see, the helmet would quickly be pitched into the snowbank. I would be flying around out there hell-bent-for-leather, the cold breeze flush against my face.

What I remember most is the sensation of being swallowed up by the surroundings—cold, crisp, clear and white. I would be by myself on the backyard rink, but it felt as though I was in the middle of nowhere. You'd gaze around and it was just a wall of white, everywhere. It was magic.

London is right in Ontario's snowbelt, and we had some winters when you couldn't even get out the front door—it was unbelievable. We had paths, cut like mazes, just to get out of the house. Our backyard was buried under an avalanche of snow. Every sound—my skates carving through the ice, a slapshot unleashed from point-blank range—echoed off the massive snowbanks around the rink. All the neighbors knew when you were out there, because they could hear everything.

It was all so condensed; everything was so simple on the ice. It was just you, your stick and a couple of pucks. The ice was crisp. My blades were sharp. The air was cool and bracing, but I felt warm. That was life.

It was as if we had our own little hockey franchise on that backyard rink. My father, Carl, was the owner, manager, rink attendant and total rink-rat. It was my home ice, but he owned it. I may have fancied myself the Rocket Richard of the place, but my Dad had built the Forum. The ice was awesome. My Dad began making backyard rinks as a kid growing up in Chatham, Ontario, and through the years he became a master at it. As I learned throughout my hockey days, my Dad would do whatever it took to keep that rink going. The ice was lightning fast. I could shoot the puck twice as fast on my backyard rink as I did in my games. The arena ice often wasn't flooded before your games and could be chipped up quite a bit by the time you took to the ice. But back at home, it was crisp and like a sheet of glass. If gardeners have green thumbs, Carl had a white thumb.

The ice would always be at its best in the morning, especially during a thaw, because it took a while for the sun to rise over the trees. I'd get out there as soon as I woke up, while my brother Brett preferred to sleep in and watch cartoons. When he finally got out there, the ice would be totally chewed up and he'd complain, "Dad, the ice is horrible." But by that time I'd already got all my skating in.

After I played shinny in the early evening with the neighborhood kids, my Dad and I would work on skills. And, much to my delight, Carl would occasionally lose track of what time a kid was supposed to go to bed. If there was ice to be had out there, that's where we both wanted to be. We worked on a lot of passing, one-time shots, tons of deflections. Our favorite drill was "skate in a circle." I would skate the circle, take a pass and shoot as quickly as possible on net. Then my Dad would get lined up to do the same thing, and I would pass to him. So I'd get my passing in. He'd get his passing in, too. Not that working on his passing mattered to him—but some days his passing could use the work, trust me. We'd have a great time.

Eventually, my Mom would be knocking on the window.

"C'mon in, guys."

I would plead in a whisper, "Dad, just a little while longer?"

"What time do you normally go to bed?" he would ask.

"Oh, in a half hour."

He would yell back, "Bon, a half hour."

When that half hour was up, I would be pressing him for another ten minutes. What was my Mom going to say? I'd be thinking, "Everyone else is in bed. Dad's on my side. This is cool." It might make me a little tired in school the next day, but that was a risk I was willing to take. I would sit there in class, yawning, and say casually to one of my classmates, "I was out until nine-thirty last night with my Dad. What time were you in bed?"

I wasn't as keen on being a good student back then, and I used to get in trouble a little bit for occasionally cutting corners in school. I remember we had this one exercise where we would have to pick out a word and write a sentence using it. Being someone who couldn't sit still for too long, finding thirty words and having to write a sentence with each wasn't too appealing. So I begged off on that assignment. But my attitude at the time was, "What are they going to do? They can't come into my house. They can't take me off my rink." I'm just a little kid thinking this stuff. It got to the point where my Mom made me do homework before I was allowed on the rink, and that gave me all the motivation I needed to get it done.

One year at school, I tried to bring my obsession with hockey into the classroom, with pretty dismal results. I did a science project on how to make a rink in Grade 3. I had cotton balls for the snow and tinfoil covered with plastic wrap so it looked like real ice. I used toothpicks to make the nets. I did it all myself and thought it was awesome, but the teacher didn't seem to agree. You were graded either 1, 2, 3 or 4, with 4 being the worst. I got a 3. A lot of dorks who had their mothers do their projects for them got higher marks. I remember being pretty ticked off about that.

I was six and a half years old when Mom decided house league hockey might be a good way for me to burn off some excess energy. I wasn't the best player in the league at all, but I slowly developed as I moved up.

That I wasn't one of the stars of the league didn't stop me from hamming it up in the backyard. I never imagined I was someone else when I was out on the backyard rink; I was always just me. I would get out there and make some nifty little play to score into the empty net and think it was great. I would raise my hands to celebrate the goal and hear the crowd going wild, and I would try to make out all the fans in the snowbank, amid the vast sea of white. I would think, "Look at me—all right! I just made this little play on this pylon. Okay, so it hasn't got a heartbeat. But what a play!" That's how you build confidence, by repeating the skills over and over so that you really believe you can do it in a game. I gained a lot of what turned into confidence on that backyard rink, knowing that I could do it. Everything progressed. Everything came from playing.

Game days held no special attraction back then; I much preferred to stay practicing on the backyard rink where I could run the show. The house league games were like a brief interruption to the more serious business at hand. My Dad would throw my skateguards on, drive me to the arena and I would dash onto the ice with the rest of my teammates. When the game was over, I couldn't wait to get back to my private haven in the backyard.

I can still remember my first house league game, when the referees came out and placed us in our positions on the ice. The ref said, "Every time I blow the whistle and we have a face-off, get your butt back here, and I want you in the same position every time." The referee was dictating everything. I can recall thinking, "Who are these guys with the stripes? They're blowing the whistle on me here. I can't shoot the puck when I want to shoot the puck. I haven't got control of this. I don't like this." It took me a while to accept it. Sitting on the bench between shifts was also a drag.

To me, the rink meant free time. I was out there a lot by myself. On Saturdays, with the exception of a break for my games, I would play for six straight hours. The other kids might have been out at afternoon shows or messing around at the local mall, but I never felt like I was missing anything. The only way someone could have convinced me to go to a matinee was by dragging me there. When you're a kid, cool is to be in control of yourself. Cool is to be doing what you want to do.

The backyard rink came complete with music, but it wasn't exactly the organ tunes you hear at Maple Leaf Gardens. I was into the heavy-metal band AC/DC when I was a kid. I had all their tapes. Everybody used to give me AC/DC tapes for Christmas and birthdays. I had a tiny radio with a little tape player, and I used to plug it in outside and let the music blare while I played. With all the snow banked around the rink, it reverberated all over the backyard; it was just like a concert. I thought it was great, though the neighbors probably didn't share my view. A lot of lyrics didn't make much sense, but it was upbeat and perfect for a little rock'n'roll hockey.

Girls were pretty far down my list at the time. When I was a kid, I never saw Wayne Gretzky or Mark Messier hanging around with their girlfriends. If the stars of the game weren't hanging around with girls, I sure wasn't going to be caught hanging around with them.

Besides, this was when I was in public school. I wasn't even sure whether I liked girls or not. The way I figured it, the other guys may be getting the babes now. So be it. I'm just going to keep practicing. I just felt there would always be time for that other stuff, but there were only so many hours that I could be on the rink.

I wasn't really thinking about being a professional hockey player at that point—I just had fun at it. The backyard rink was a chance to go out and be by myself. The games provided me with the opportunity to use the skills I was practicing and to see what I had within myself. I thrived on the competition. Even as a little kid, I loved to win. I didn't think too much about the future, I just prepared myself for each year of hockey. I really had no idea where my love for the game would take me. But I was eager to find out.

2

A Real Corker

OTHER VOICES:

Bonnie Lindros

The clanging of metal echoed up the stairs and I jumped out of bed to investigate. It could only be one of two things: a crazed intruder or Eric the Terror. As I suspected, it was the latter.

I saw the culprit the second I reached the kitchen doorway. There was two-year-old Eric, looking angelic with his fair hair and chubby cheeks, standing on a stool and leaning over the stove with a wooden spoon clutched in his hand. He had taken all of the elements out of the electric stove and put them on top. He was stirring all this metal with the wooden spoon and the spoon was on fire! I nearly had a heart attack.

"What are you doing, Eric?"

"I'm cooking."

He was in constant motion as a child. You were always trying to anticipate what he was going to do next. When you have your second and third kids, you know. But with your first, you never know what they've got in their bag of tricks. And Eric's bag was certainly overflowing. Our doctor back in London used to say, "If you can get him through his first three years without having his stomach pumped, you deserve a medal."

One time, I was on the phone and Eric wanted my attention. He soon found a way to get it. When I wasn't looking, he climbed onto the chair in the dining room, grabbed hold of the curtains and tried to swing across like Tarzan. I had to excuse myself from the phone because the curtains were torn right off the dining-room wall.

He was a real corker. He still is. That's his personality.

Taking him to the doctor's office was always an adventure. He couldn't sit still for a second. He'd be looking at a book. Then he'd be looking at the aquarium. And then he'd be talking to all the ladies in the waiting room. He'd say, "What do you think's the matter with her, Mom?" And then he'd have to check it out himself.

Our doctor was a really jovial guy. Since I worked in Emergency at Victoria Hospital, I had a good idea of who the best doctors were, and I was convinced ours was at the top of the list. He was a little on the chubby side, so Carl's nickname for him was "Old Fat Butt." We were just kids ourselves then. After one appointment, Carl said to me, "How's Old Fat Butt?" So on the next visit, Eric trots in to see the doctor and he says, "Hi, Fat Butt." The poor doctor pretended he didn't hear him. Carl and I had a long talk about what we said in front of the kids after that. I hope Dr. Keith Johnson can laugh at this now.

Eric was let loose on the world on Wednesday, February 28, 1973, at 8:10 PM. He was supposed to be a Valentine's Day baby, but he was two weeks late. Eric was born at the hospital where I worked, so they rolled out the red carpet for us. Our obstetrician was a great guy, Dr. John Collins. I remember Carl coming into the delivery room just before Eric was born. He was wearing one of those hospital scrub suits with a drawstring on the bottoms. The delivery room had swinging doors. Carl came through the doors and then he looked down because his underwear was showing at the drawstring. As he glanced down, the swinging doors were flung open by someone rushing through from the other side, knocking Carl halfway across the room. Trying to regain his composure, Carl said, "We may begin now."

Eric didn't cry, he just blinked in the light. I had been praying for a girl; I wanted a girl so much, because I knew I'd have boys. Carl comes from a family of all boys, so I was hoping our first child would be a girl. Carl was hoping for a boy, but he didn't dare say it out loud.

Eric was just a tiny, pink thing with dimples in his cheeks and chin. He had light-brown hair and he was really wrinkled because he was overdue. He weighed seven pounds, one and a half ounces, and was twenty and a half inches long. My parents were with us at the hospital. They had postponed their trip to Florida until Eric was born. Carl was really excited, but my Mom had some sobering words for the proud Papa: "You've got no idea what a difference this kid's going to make in your life."

We chose the name Eric because we wanted a Scandinavian name to match our last name. We were told Eric meant "kingly." I wanted a name that you couldn't shorten because I'm famous for shortening names. Eric's middle name is the same as Carl's, Bryan.

When Eric was a baby, even pushing him down the sidewalk in his buggy proved challenging. He always grabbed the sides of the buggy and stood up and held on to the hood so he could see out. He had to see where he was going. I'd spend my whole time turning him around and laying him down. Eric still doesn't like lying down.

The first time he walked was at my friend Donna Stewart's farmhouse outside of Chatham. He was seven and a half months old, but had really sturdy legs for a little guy. Donna had a Fisher-Price "popcorn popper" that her kids used to push around. Eric was holding onto the couch and pushing the toy with his other hand. Soon, he didn't realize he wasn't holding the couch any more because he was concentrating so hard. He wasn't thinking about what he was doing. He forgot he wasn't supposed to be letting go of the couch. Donna came into the room and screamed, "The baby's walking!" Eric looked at her with a shocked look on his face, thought something was wrong and sat right down. About ten days later, Eric tried again, and he was off and running shortly after that.

Most babies at that stage would be safe in a playpen if you wanted to leave the room, but not Eric. We heard something moving in the house one night and thought somebody might have broken in. We thought, "Uh-oh, what's happening?" And there was this little shuffling fool entering our room in his yellow Dr. Dentons. He was so short you could hardly see him over the mattress. I said, "Carl, I think he's out of his crib." He had stacked all his teddies up and climbed over the side. He had this huge canopy crib, but he still got out.

He would get up every day at five-thirty in the morning. On the odd day, he would sleep until seven. I was praying some days he would sleep until nine, but he never did. He was a good sleeper. But when he was up, he was up. And we were all up.

Our babysitter in London, Susan Eynon, found the best method to keep Eric occupied was to put him in the bathtub with all his toys, because then he couldn't get away. He was happy to do that. He still loves baths, but now, instead of playing with toys, he reads. That's his ritual. They all fight for the tubs in our house.

I tried to keep Eric in nighties and booties and make him look like a baby, but he didn't act like one. One of my neighbors from London said to me once that she couldn't remember him ever being a baby. That really upset me—I wanted him to be a baby.

You just knew he was going to be big. When he was three years old he had tremendous hands and tremendous feet. By the time he was seven and a half he had hands the size of an adult. We used to take photocopies of them. His Uncle Paul said he was just like a puppy with big paws.

Eric got his first set of stitches long before he set foot on a hockey rink. He was standing at the back door when his shoes slipped on a wooden ledge and he went crashing down. I just died. He was only eleven months and he had to get stitches over his left eye. His second set of stitches came shortly after that when we were at my friend's house and he flipped over the runners of her rocking chair while he was whipping around. You have to remember, he had the motor skills to do all these things but he didn't have the brains.

Toys held little attraction for Eric as a kid. He had a Fisher-Price phone and a xylophone and he liked those, but his favorite pastime was to sit on the floor and bang on pots and pans and cans of food.

He had good fine-motor skills and liked to hook rugs. He could sew really well. In Grade 7, he had to make place mats for home economics. They only had to make four for the class, so I made two more on my own to complete the set. Although I hate to admit it, his were better than mine. His sister Robin got a rug-hooking kit for Christmas last year and she wasn't too keen about it, but Eric could hardly wait for her to open the box.

Eric's birthdays were another matter entirely—he was just awful. He would get so excited and his ultra-competitive nature would shine through, turning the jelly-bean hunts into a war. I remember 'fth birthday I spanked him and put him to bed right at his party. Some of the kids had found more jelly beans than he had and he couldn't handle it. The next year we stressed cooperative games, but I still used to shudder on the day of his birthday party.

When he played sports, Eric liked to play with the older kids. When he played with his own peer group, he would be very upset with their level of play. The hardest year for Eric was when he was in kindergarten and the kids that he played with were in Grade 1. They were in school all day and he was only in school a half-day. Once he entered Grade 1, he was fine, because then he could play with everyone. He had a couple of friends but he has never been a real social butterfly. He's a little quieter than that, really. Even now, he still prefers a casual situation; he doesn't like to be on display. He just likes to sit in the kitchen and chat, eat and watch TV.

He always liked to play with his cousin Brian because Brian is five years older and Eric could play road hockey with him and his friends. One of Brian's friends once hit Eric in the face with his stick because he didn't like the idea that this little kid was better than him at hockey. Eric was so competitive that a lot of times he would step on people's toes. Sometimes he knew he was doing it, but he didn't care. He was going to get what he wanted and what he was focused on. I'd say it was a two-way thing. Part of it was that people felt threatened by Eric, and part of it was that Eric really meant to threaten them.

He was never part of the "in" crowd, and I think that drove him to achieve so that people would respect him. He didn't have the most friends at school, but he would try to gain the approval of his peers by showing them he could play ball better or get a higher mark on the tests. I think his attitude was that they might not like him, but they had to respect him.

Eric is really into rules. Even when he was little, that was the routine we kept him on. He knew what the rules were and he followed them. He didn't have outer limits, so we tried to make outer limits for him. If he knew the rules and he lived within the rules, then everything was cool. But if he stepped out, well then . . .

It was clear to Eric that if I said something, I meant it. If he didn't comply, there were serious repercussions—SERIOUS. Sometimes when his friends were over, I had to tell them not to do something, and Eric would say, "And she means it. So if you do it, you know there'll be trouble." Because Eric was so hard to handle, he had to know, then and there, it was not going to work. I would say, "Eric, stop doing that. I told you not to three times. You're getting spanked." After his spanking, Eric would announce that it didn't hurt, but we noticed that he never did it again.

Eric was initially thrilled when his brother Brett arrived on the scene. It was just three months shy of his third birthday. When we arrived home with the baby, we gave Eric a little Viewmaster and told him it was from his new brother. Whenever we took pictures of the baby, he would get out his little Viewmaster and he'd be clicking away, too. As soon as Brett gave Eric his present, Eric immediately gave him his own prized blanket.

But there was still an adjustment period he had to go through with baby brother around now, cutting in on the limelight. One day Carl's mom, Marg, who was helping me out at home with the two kids, had baked a chocolate cake. We were sitting upstairs in our sunroom while Eric kept himself busy in the kitchen. A little too busy. He got his hands on a spatula and decided to start serving up the cake. He flipped it all over the ceiling and the walls— the entire kitchen was covered in chocolate cake. We didn't yell, we just looked at it. Carl's mom said, "I don't think he's really accepted the baby yet." Eric loved Brett, but he didn't like the idea of losing his unique position in our home.

Eric was keen about skating right away. When he was one and a half, we got him a pair of bobskates. They had little straps. It ~~would~~ be freezing cold in London and his bobskates would be ~~'~~s boots all the time, so we bought some hockey laces and wrapped them around the skates so that they would stay on for the duration of the afternoon. With the bobskates being 88 cents on sale, I think the laces cost more than the skates. He was just thrilled with skating. He was basically walking around, but he thought he was awesome.

I signed him up for skating lessons before he was five and then house league hockey when he was six and a half years old, hoping it would keep him occupied for a bit and use up some of his boundless energy. A lot of his friends were joining and he wanted to play with the other kids. Carl said he would be too big for hockey, but I said, "I don't care. He's driving me crazy." I didn't realize it was going to be the best thing to happen to him. It gave him something to focus on. All his energy could be channeled into something that was positive.

One of the only things I remember about Eric's first year of hockey is Carl carrying him into the arena with his skates on so that we didn't have to leave for the rink until the last minute. I used to take a little chair for Brett to stand on, as most London arenas had terrific ice surfaces but no bleachers. Eric's motor skills were good. He seemed to recognize how to change the things he was doing wrong. He didn't shake the earth, let me tell you. But he liked it, and that was all that counted.

OTHER VOICES:

Carl Lindros

On the ice at skating lessons, Eric was like a little firefly scooting all over the place. He was underaged for the group he was in.

The class was for five-year-olds and older, and he wouldn't turn five for another six months. I'm sure the teacher knew it, but she just got a kick out of him. He finished all four skating levels in that program—which many kids enjoy until they're ten years old—by the time he was five. The final class was on his fifth birthday. He was razzing his instructor, Betty, and saying, "How old do you think I am?" She knew he was young because of his attention span and lack of patience in waiting his turn. He would be fooling around and not watching until finally she would say, "Okay Eric, do it." He would get out there and start swirling around, and it was all Betty could do not to burst out laughing.

Bonnie was the one who really got him into these programs and took him there. At that time, I was work, work, work. Hockey wasn't high on my list of things for the kids to get involved with. I felt at the time that hockey didn't fit well with schooling, and to me, the way hockey was being run at that time wasn't all that desirable. In my mind, I thought that basketball or perhaps football might be sports where you could play, have the fun of being involved on a team and be successful at school. My feeling was that sometimes if you get to be too big physically in hockey and your skill level doesn't keep pace with your growth, then you could get slotted in as an enforcer. In actual fact, perhaps I made that conclusion because I didn't cut the mustard as a hockey player. I had what they call "stone hands." If I got twenty points a season, it was something. It seemed odd because when I played basketball I could control the ball and make all kinds of passes. But I could never do it in hockey. Maybe I didn't practice enough.

When Bonnie enrolled Eric in the Red Circle house league, I made the rounds with him and our neighbor, Ted Ralph, and his son Edward to pick up the equipment they would need. Bonnie equipped us with the local *Shopper's News* and she'd circled all the ̶ ̶ ̶used equipment. There were some garage sales and there ̶ment exchanges run by the local hockey association and one at a shoe-repair shop. We had already paid two dollars for his first pair of real skates and, fortunately, there were a lot of bargains to be had on equipment, since he would no doubt be outgrowing it all quite soon.

Eric and Edward would go to each of the houses. Edward would get first choice at one house and Eric would get first choice at the next. It was all antique. The shoulder pads looked like little football ones. None of the stuff matched. I'm not even sure if the shin pads were a complete set. I don't think it cost much more than twelve dollars for the first set of equipment. We bought Eric a really good new helmet, and we also got him new socks and a sweater in Montreal Canadiens' colors, because that's what he liked. He wouldn't take the helmet off; he kept it on all day long. He even wore it while he was riding his bike. The only time he took it off was when he ate. The rest of the time he pranced around in his hockey equipment. He was really keen for it.

I offered to help coach his team that first year with the Red Circle Minor Hockey Association. There were three lines, and all you had to do was change them when the buzzer went. There wasn't a whole lot to it. I knew a little bit more about it than some of the other parents at the time. I thought, "Well, you've got to put something into the system if you're going to get something out of it." It got going on a very low-key basis and it was a lot of fun. We held a barbeque at our house at the end of the season, and one of the families brought a cake shaped like an ice rink, complete with the players.

As soon as Eric got home from each game, he'd get out in the backyard rink and go skating again for hours. He would mentally replay the game on the ice in the backyard. He loved it.

I made Eric's first backyard rink when he was nearly three. I had always made rinks when I was a kid myself, which was tough in Chatham because the winter would only be cold enough for a rink for maybe two weeks at a time. Very often, the ice wasn't good enough to skate on, so we would play road hockey on it. Still, the backyard rinks would get bigger every year. My brother Paul and I followed the theory that you got a better surface if you used hot water. We'd hook up the hose downstairs in the furnace room and just empty the hot-water tank. The steam would just be spewing off. I don't have any idea if it did work better, but we always insisted on using the hot water, much to my mother's dismay.

They used to let us into the Senior A hockey games for free in Chatham if we helped out with resurfacing the ice between periods, so I picked up a little experience that way, too. They didn't have a Zamboni back then, so all the kids lined up in a row with shovels to form a human Zamboni and went around the entire ice surface. We also took turns pulling the barrel filled with hot water that was used to flood the ice—we certainly earned the price of admission.

Hockey Night in Canada was a big deal in the Lindros household—it was quite the family occasion. My brother Paul and I would have to sit through *The Lawrence Welk Show* with Grandma before the hockey game came on. We would dance with her while Lawrence Welk performed those grand old favorites, and Grandma loved it. Afterwards, she'd sit there and turn a blind eye while we devoured more than a half gallon of ice cream while watching the hockey game. It was sort of a pact.

We also had night hockey on our backyard rink in Chatham. Well, sort of. There was a big row of windows across the back of the house, so we would go up in the second story of our home and flip on every light to try to light the rink. Paul and I weren't very energy-conscious, that's for sure. The lights weren't really effective, though. You could only see shadows, but I think it was part of the fun.

. . . . .uties of hockey is that kids get exposed to a real
. . . . .nadians. It breaks down the pockets we live in

in the bigger cities. If you come from a well-to-do family, that means nothing when you're on the ice. You can't hide in hockey. I think hockey really provides an opportunity to have a sense of the Canadian mosaic. It gives kids a chance to appreciate the family environment some of their teammates come from, because very often you end up having a sleepover or traveling to tournaments together. I think it helps the kids to see qualities in others, both positive and negative. The vehicle in this case is hockey, but the vehicle could just as easily be being a member of a band or the Boy Scouts.

When Eric first started to play hockey, I had a tendency to start bombarding him with pointers immediately after a game. I went from having absolutely no interest in hockey at all to, once it was a go, it being a project where I just went nuts. Bonnie noticed Eric was really happy when he came out of the arena, but after our little chat on the way home he would turn very serious and start thinking about all the things he could improve on. It didn't seem as much fun for him at that point. Bon then suggested that we take two cars to the rink—and that I travel solo. She was dead on. I quickly got the message.

It took me a while to learn that the best thing to do after a game is to identify a couple of good things that they did and give them a pat on the back. You don't really get into analyzing "Why didn't you do this?" and "Why didn't you do that?"

After the backyard rink melted, we would sometimes get up early to go to Victoria Park in London for a little shinny. It was an outdoor public rink and you weren't supposed to be out there with sticks, but we would be out there at 6:30 AM when nobody else was around, so I don't think anyone really minded. You would get some good exercise, go home and have a nice breakfast, and away you would go to work. You felt great. I'm not sure who enjoyed that more, Eric or myself.

Gaye Black (Eric's aunt)

Eric was always into hockey, even when he was still in diapers. I remember at his first Christmas, we were all at my mother's place opening our presents. My son Brian, who was five at the time, got a little hockey stick as one of his gifts, but he buried it behind the Christmas tree in the basement rec room because he didn't like it. Well, that was all Eric needed to see. He climbed behind the tree, grabbed the hockey stick and ran—he didn't walk or stumble or stagger—he RAN all through the basement with this stick like he'd died and gone to heaven. He was less than ten months old at the time.

As a toddler, Eric was constantly tearing around and banging into things. He would end up with black eyes and stitches, but it never slowed him down. It reached the point where if you were arranging a family portrait you had to work it in between Eric's assorted cuts and bruises. He didn't worry about hurting himself, though. He was always going full tilt.

My sister Bonnie was also quite a handful as a youngster. So after Eric came along and gave her all she could handle—and sometimes more—we would tell her, "Well, you deserve it." But there were some days when Bonnie was near tears and saying "What am I doing wrong? Why is this kid *always* a handful?" Some kids are easier than others, and he was not easy. To keep him from getting into trouble, she had to give him so many activities. He was one of those kids who just pressed you all the time.

Lynn Vanderaa (family friend)

My son Mark and Eric became buddies when they played on the same hockey team one year in London. They were nine years old. It was Eric's first year of competitive hockey. Eric was over at our place a lot, and even after they moved to Toronto he usually came to stay with us for a week or two every summer. We had a pool at our apartment, and when they were downstairs doing their lengths, you always knew that if somebody did 100, Eric would have to do 130.

Eric doesn't know his own limitations. As far as he's concerned, he doesn't have any. He has what you call a lot of gears. He always seems to be able to notch it up another level when his team needs him. Eric is the type of boy who would die at the end of a race, giving every last ounce trying to win.

He had a lot of character even as a kid. I'll never forget what he did at the London minor hockey banquet at the end of that season he and Mark played together. The boys had been defensive partners. Bonnie had nicknamed Eric "Loosey Goosey" and Mark was "Steady Eddie." Bonnie gave Eric his nickname because the minute the puck was dropped he was nowhere near playing defense. He ran the whole ice. Poor Mark had to guard the nest. He was Mr. Save-the-Bacon. Well, on awards day, Eric scooped up just about everything, including the trophy for leading scorer. What really stands out in my mind is that he got up in front of an auditorium full of adults and kids and said, "I just can't accept this by myself, because without Mark being back there to take care of the fort, I couldn't have got all these goals and assists." He said, "Mark, you've got to come up here and share this with me."

For a ten-year-old kid to stand up there and say that was really something special. To be honest with you, whether Mark had been there on defense with him or not would not have made one iota of difference. The bottom line was that Eric was recognizing Mark. I don't know very many people who would share a trophy with somebody else, even as adults.

You could always expect the unexpected from Eric. You would never, ever really know—and I don't think even Eric knows—what he's really capable of.

3

Family Ties

Shinny hockey on the local public rink can be a little chippy at times, but this was getting ridiculous.

My younger brother Brett, my Dad and I had made tracks to a nearby outdoor rink in Toronto for some shinny action on a Saturday afternoon. As was usually the case, the place was packed. As was also usually the case, there were a few guys carrying on as if they were the lords of the rink. They just thought they were great. Now, we're good players, we know we're good players, but we don't fly through everyone and act like we own the ice. On this particular afternoon, there were a couple of demented guys skating around jabbing everyone with their sticks.

We knew there was potential for trouble, because if someone stuck me, I'd stick him back. And if someone stuck my brother, my brother would stick him back. It got to the point where this big guy was taking runs at Brett and me, but he was gunning for my little brother in particular. After he bashed Brett on one play, I hit him, and then he hit me back.

It wasn't long before my Dad arrived on the scene to straighten things out. It was very verbal and a little physical—Dad basically took him apart. Needless to say, this guy didn't try anything again.

No one messes around with my brother when he's on the ice with me. No one messes with me when I'm on the ice with my Dad. If my sister Robin's got a problem and my brother's in the same school, no one messes around with my sister. And no one messes around with Mom. You touch one, you touch us all. It's the best backup anyone could have.

I think our attitude comes from being a very athletic family. Athletics breed a certain person. They breed a certain competitiveness, a certain desire to win, a certain fear of failure—and the recognition that hard work is the building block of success.

My parents are hard-working people. My Dad's a chartered accountant and my Mom's a registered nurse. They didn't inherit tons of money; they had to apply themselves. And whatever they have, they've earned.

I think I just picked up on that. I've always been willing to work for what I got. I think if you do anything, you should do your best. It's a family philosophy: you don't get ahead sitting down waiting for somebody to do something for you.

I've got a great relationship with my parents. It's sort of neat the way everything evolves. My parents have always tried to instill confidence in us; they never talk down to us. I get a kick out of referring to my parents by their first names instead of "Mom" and "Dad." It started about a year and a half ago. My friend Jeff Hardy would say, "We're going to go talk to Ian." I'd say, "Who's Ian?" He'd say, "My Dad. We'll see what Big Ian has to say." So I started saying, "We're going to talk to Big Carl, see what's up on the home front with Big Carl." I refer to them as Mom and Dad about 65 or 70 percent of the time. But around friends I call them "Big Carl" and "Bon."

My parents are very level-headed. They don't get caught up in money and they have their own keen sense of what's important to them. My Mom is very outspoken, while my Dad thinks a lot; he's always thinking. Not to say that Mom doesn't think, she just doesn't keep as much inside. She says what she thinks. Bon's been known to go a little too far once in a while, but that's why my Mom and my Dad are a really good balance. My Mom's the jumper; my Dad's always got the backup plan. My Mom's got the ideas running; my Dad will take the ideas and make calculated decisions from them.

My Mom was the one who had to cut through the stuff or nothing would get done. Dad was the relaxed guy, a little more laid-back. But at times, Carl was the one you'd avoid and Bon was the one you would go to. You had to work it out, but luckily you had two personalities you could work with.

Mom was really the iron hand when I was growing up, and if it got really bad, my Dad would hop in. I didn't want that. Joke around with Dad, but don't mess around with the discipline. My Mom used to buy a pile of wooden spoons, and she didn't use them just for cooking. It got to the point where Brett and I would try to scatter them in hiding places all over the house. Anything you could get yourself in trouble with, I was there. I spent so much time in the corner as a kid that my parents were sure my face was going to grow V-shaped.

Bon believed in punishments that were here and now. One time I really got myself in her bad books and she declared, "I just don't know what punishment suits this behavior." Good ol' brother Brett, ever the helpful one, starts coughing and mutters under his breath, "Toilet bowls. Toilet bowls." Guess what I wound up scrubbing.

We always did work for our misdeeds; we never got banished to our rooms, where we could sit and relax. Dishes were another chore you could get saddled with. If we were sitting at the table eating dinner and Mom was exhausted from working, she would say, "Boy, I'm really tired tonight. I hope someone misbehaves." She was never disappointed. We couldn't restrain ourselves. Mom would say, "Who's got dirty fingernails tonight?" We'd start having a fit because we knew that meant someone would be doing the dishes.

I never watched a lot of television when I was a kid, and I hardly ever read. It was just me and the rink. My Mom was always pushing me to read books; she spent a lot of time reading to me when I was young. I liked *Lassie Come Home*—except that Mom used to cry so hard when she read it to me that she could hardly get through 'it. Not surprisingly, I liked books about hockey. I also liked stories that were offbeat. In one of my favorite kids' books, there were some church mice that thought they'd built a flying saucer. They thought they were going to the moon on this flying saucer, but they really hadn't left the church vestry, and the choir was getting ready for a performance. The one section I loved was when this big, fat guy was bending over getting his choir outfit on. The story said, "Behold the moon." The mice thought they were approaching the moon, and it was this guy's butt. That was the kind of stuff I liked. I liked the stories where kids got into a lot of trouble—I'd laugh my head off. I loved it when somebody else was getting into trouble besides me.

Mom had her work cut out feeding our gang. I had an impressive appetite as a kid, and my favorite was peanut-butter-and-jam sandwiches—the dentist's delight. I grew up on those. I didn't like the health food peanut butter, it had to have sugar in it. One day I forgot my lunch when I was in Grade 7 and my Mom brought it over to the school. She used to put our lunches in plastic grocery bags, because the paper bags would break. It was my usual light lunch: five sandwiches, two fruits, two juice boxes, some cookies, and celery sticks with peanut butter. It was quite a bagful. The teacher held up my lunch in front of the class and she said, "Eric, are you sharing this with the whole class or are we thinking of sending it to the Third World?" It's a wonder I didn't bankrupt the family; the groceries were always at least $200 a crack.

My brother Brett and I fought a lot. He used to do things that would drive me up the wall; he just knew how to get under my skin. He's nearly three years younger than I am, but he was an expert at manipulating my Mom from an early age. He could do it even at four years old. My brother would smack himself and wail, "Mom, he hit me!" And it would be, "Eric, get to your room!" We'd play downstairs and we'd get into a fight, and he would have her wrapped around his finger. It wasn't until years later that she began to realize that Dennis the Menace was responsible as much—if not more—than I was.

I used to chase him all over the house. The chandeliers would shake. He'd go flying into the bathroom and lock the door. Then he'd come out and I'd be hiding behind something and he would bolt to another bathroom. The bathroom was home free. It was a game, but it could get pretty rough.

We've always shared a room. We're kind of like the Odd Couple—Brett's neat, I'm a little sloppy. Okay, maybe more than a little. One time, on his way home from school, Bubba spots one of those huge cardboard boxes from a refrigerator and carts it home with him. (I had different nicknames for him: "Bubba," "the Bart Man," "Bartlett.") Well, Bubba grabs the cardboard box, splits it up to make a divider and tapes lines across the middle of the room. His side was supposed to be off-limits, but it was tough for him to enforce. I'd say, "Well, Brett, I'm coming over," and then I'd stick my foot over on his side just to get him mad.

My Mom made us switch sides of the room because mine was such a mess. I used to be nearest to the door, but she decided against that. Brett's bed is now closest to the door, so that when guests are walking by they see the nice part and I'm hidden away on the other side. You couldn't see the floor on my side. I always used to work on Brett's desk, because mine was usually buried under a pile of rubble. I guess I haven't become much neater through the years. Shortly after I returned home at the end of last season, Bon had me straightening up the mess under my bed.

"I'm going to have a maid some day," I yelled from under the bed.

"No you won't, Eric Lindros. You're too cheap," Bon replied.

We both just started laughing.

When we were little kids back in London, Mom used to hire a babysitter once a week to look after us while she took a tennis lesson. One week, Mom phoned to check up on things while she was out. She couldn't hear us in the background, so she thought something was up, because you could *always* hear us in the background. We would be whipping around, screaming and making lots of noise. Bon decided to come home to investigate, and when she got home, I was in the closet and Brett was in bed. The babysitter wanted to watch some soap opera; I wanted to watch *Sesame Street*. So I was in the closet doing a slow boil, and the babysitter had put Brett to bed. Mom quit tennis.

Brett and I used to play on the backyard rink together, but we almost always ended up fighting. He had a lot of friends; I didn't have that many. He would have a friend over on the rink and it just wouldn't work. He would want control, and I wasn't about to give it to him.

Still, it was a different story when someone tried to lay a beating on my brother. I might beat on him, but no one else was going to. Once, when he was in Grade 6 and I was in Grade 8, he and his buddies got into trouble with some skinhead-wannabes. One of my brother's friends told one of these characters he dressed like a cow because he was wearing black clothes with white socks. The next thing they knew, this group of skinheads was out to kick their butts. Our schools were right beside each other, and word traveled fast. As soon as I heard about it, I came over to escort Brett home. When the skinheads saw they wouldn't be dealing just with a kid several years younger, they had a change of heart.

The Bart Man's developing into quite a hockey player. If he wants it, he's got a very good shot at a professional career. But no one's going to make it easy for him. I went to a couple of Brett's games last year. The refs always pick on him. It's the same stuff I go through, but sometimes I deserve it. Well, a lot of times I deserve it.

It was really bad for him in high school hockey at St. Michael's College School last year. He was only in Grade 10, and he made the senior team at the start of the season, even though they weren't really expecting him to make it. But he was a marked man and he got into a fight nearly every game. He played in only three of the six exhibition games because he was suspended from the other three for fighting. In his last game before he had to decide whether he was going to play senior or junior, the biggest player from the other team jumped him along the boards in the closing minutes and tried to beat him up. Although this player was four years older, Brett was able to spin him around, flip his helmet off and pin him to the ice. If he wanted to, Brett could have pummeled him. Meanwhile, one of Brett's teammates came up and started ridiculing the opposing player by chanting in his ear, "You know, he's only fourteen." The fans from the other high school then congregated at the boards and started yelling at him to beat the crap out of Brett. This player just flipped out. As Brett and my Dad were trying to leave the arena, this guy's brother and some of his football buddies followed them out and starting rocking the car. My Dad got out of the car—all six-foot-five of him—and these clowns quickly realized they didn't want to mess around with him. In the end, Brett decided to play junior, because playing senior just wasn't worth the hassle.

It isn't easy for him being "Eric's little brother." A lot of things might open up for him, but it's a tough road in a lot of ways. It's as though I'm the builder and he's the brand new car riding on my road, getting there, but getting dirty at the same time.

Brett doesn't like to have things given to him. He likes to earn everything he gets, which is the perfect attitude. I used to drive him to school once in a while and I would ask if he had lunch money. He'd say Mom had packed his lunch, but I'd hand him a few bucks anyway. He'd reject it with a scowl. "I don't want your money." The next thing I turn around and he's selling my memorabilia. But that's my brother—he'll get you one way or another.

My little sister Robin's great. I'm pretty protective of her, and she looks after me. If someone in the stands is giving me a rough time during a game, she'll let them have it with both barrels. She's not afraid to yap. She's just a little thing, but she's been hanging around us, and our vocabulary at times has slipped. So Robin can really let loose.

When my parents were preparing to adopt Robin, the agency sent out a social worker to check out the situation. They wanted to see whether Mom and Dad were appropriate parents. The lady from the agency decided to spend a little time with me to see if I was a well-adjusted child.

I was four and a half at the time and was really into putting on my own circus. Well, I took this lady downstairs so that I could perform for her "under the Big Top." First of all, I had the top hat and I sold some tickets at the front wicket. Then I did all the acts. I juggled. I did cartwheels. I pretended I was the lion-tamer. Of course, I also had to pretend I was the lion. I was the master of ceremonies. I just whipped around and did the whole thing. The lady went upstairs and collapsed into a chair. She was wiped out.

My Mom asked, "Adjusted?"

"Adjusted," gasped the social worker.

I think *she* had to be adjusted later.

When I was younger, a lot of the kids at school picked on Robin quite a bit, and I fought a lot about that because I wouldn't let them get away with it. Now that she's older, Robin's quite capable of sticking up for herself. She has that Lindros feistiness when she needs it. She used to say, "My big brother will beat you up." Now she says, "You be careful because I can really punch."

The kids at her school used to send her home with handfuls of hockey cards for me to autograph, until the principal cracked down on that. Robin has some cards that I gave her and she's really careful about where she stores them. She keeps them buried away in a special hiding place in her room and she won't let her friends in there. I gave her my Ontario Hockey League All-Star sweater, and she used to wear it sometimes to my Oshawa Generals games. It always made a big hit. People would come up and ask, "Where can we buy one of those?" Robin would reply with a big grin, "You can't." She loved to tell them that.

Robin's as busy with sports as Brett and I ever were. She takes swimming lessons and likes gymnastics, water-skiing and down-hill skiing. When I'm home from hockey, I often pick her up from Girl Guides or swimming, or help out with some of her home-work. She likes going with me for rides in the car, undoubtedly because we both love going fast with the rock'n'roll at full blast. If I don't remember to use my turn signals, Robin is the first to let me know about it. We go out and get a yogurt cone once in a while for a little treat. We just have a lot of fun together.

Our family tree is filled with athletes. My Mom's sister Marcia held the high school shot-put record in the British Common-wealth for ten years. My Dad's brother Paul played on a Vanier

Cup champion team while playing Canadian college football at Queen's University. My Mom's parents met while competing at a track-and-field meet in Chatham. And my Grandmother Marg's father competed in baseball, boxing and barrel-jumping.

I guess you could say a lot of it is in the genes. My father is six-foot-five. My mother is five-foot-eleven. Farm communities have big kids—must be the air. My parents were both athletes-of-the-year at their high school in Chatham. My father was in the Chicago Blackhawks' farm system for a short stint and was drafted by the Edmonton Eskimos of the Canadian Football League. My mother was an excellent high school basketball player and a standout in track and field.

My Dad was an absolutely natural athlete. There was nothing he tried that he didn't pick up very quickly. He was good at everything he touched—basketball, football, track and field, baseball and tennis. He was captain of the high school basketball team. He played middle linebacker and quarterback on the high school football team (though not at the same time. Dad was quite an athlete, but there are limits).

Carl's the type of guy who can walk into a room and trip over six things, but you put him on a tennis court and he's like a cat. My Grandmother Marg says he always moved before he thought. In baseball, when he heard he made the local all-star team, he just came flying out the front door, jumped down the front steps and sprained his ankle. When my Dad had his tonsils out at seventeen, my grandparents went over to the hospital to pick him up. Nobody at the hospital could find him—he had started walking home by himself. Dad doesn't sit still. He's got two speeds: he's either going full tilt or he's asleep.

He's always been a risk-taker. When he went to St. Catharines to try out for the Blackhawks' farm team, he was sixteen. Dad went more for the life experience than a shot at an NHL career. He can still vividly recall going up to Bobby Hull's hotel room with a buddy to meet "the Golden Jet." The big guns from the NHL team stayed in the same place as the farmhands. Bobby Hull was lying on the bed with his arms behind his head, and Dad says it seemed as if Hull's chest stretched from one side of the bed to the other.

It didn't take Carl long to find out what the Chicago brass had in store for him. In one of his first scrimmages, they told him to have a fight with Ken Hodge, one of the veterans on the team. Then, in their opening exhibition game, they gave him orders to go after Pete Mahovlich. Dad says that wasn't so bad, because Mahovlich couldn't fight either. It was clear that, because of his size, they wanted him to be a goon. And he wanted no part of that.

He called home and said he was thinking about leaving the team. But my Grandfather Ed suggested he stay until after the final cuts, so that no one could say he wasn't good enough. Dad made the team, but he just packed all of his gear in a green duffle bag and returned home on the bus. My Dad has never said much about his hockey experience. He never talked about the fighting. He'd rather talk about scoring—but that's a pretty brief topic on his list.

My Grandmother thought Carl would have a big adjustment coming back to high school, because there was a lot of attention in the local paper about him trying out for the Hawks. But it was a smooth transition. When he came back, he was quite convinced that being a hockey player wasn't going to be his life. He just didn't like what he saw.

My Dad made the varsity football team at the University of Western Ontario as a freshman. He was a tight end. When he got drafted by Edmonton after his final year, Mom begged him to give pro football a try. She thought it would be a neat adventure for a year. But Dad couldn't be persuaded. The average CFL salary at the time was about $7,200. He said, "If you think I'm going to put my life on the line for $7,200, I've got news for you."

He bore down hard in school. While he was at Western, he made the dean's list. My Dad's a grinder—he can grind it out for hours. The bigger the challenge, the harder he works. He just forms a mental picture of the task ahead and away he goes. He's very competitive and he's very focused. He became a partner in his firm, Peat Marwick Thorne, at the age of thirty.

Mom was an excellent athlete in her own right while growing up in Chatham. She played guard on her high school basketball team and was one of the aces on the squad. They had a powerful team. She never really got the chance to develop to her full potential, though, because there wasn't too much emphasis on women's sports at the time. When she played basketball, they could only take three steps before they had to pass. The team's uniforms were one-piece cotton bloomers with short sleeves and elastic legs, with buttons down the front and a little cotton belt. Bon says it was absolutely the ugliest thing you ever saw. It sounds like it. My Dad and the rest of the boys would trot in after the girls' games outfitted in satin shorts with contrasting trim and satin jackets with huge crests. The thrust was obviously not on the female athlete at that time.

Bon was an awesome standing broad jumper, but her specialty in track was sprinting. She always ran the anchor leg on the relay team. One time, at a big race in Ridgetown, she got so excited before she received the baton that she peed her bloomers. When she got the baton, she took off like a flash. Whoosh! All you could see was this navy bum. After she crossed the finish line, she bolted straight into the bathroom. Everyone was so thrilled because the relay team had broken the inter-county record, and Mom wasn't even around to enjoy it. But she had obviously been pumped up for the race.

Mom is ever the competitor. When I was playing hockey in London one year, they had a skating race for the parents at Christmas. Well, Bon decided she was going to win this race. And she was winning it, until one of her figure skate picks hooked on the ice and she went crashing down. She hurt her knee so badly that she could hardly walk that Christmas. Mom wasn't too fond of skating after that. She remembered how much it hurt to hit that ice. She would venture onto the backyard rink every now and then, but the fact that I was always firing pucks at her blades usually dissuaded her from staying out too long.

Mom and Dad were high school sweethearts. They had their first dance together after a track-and-field meet in Dresden, a little town outside of Chatham. Bonnie Roszell was in Grade 9, Carl Lindros was in Grade 10. Dad was quite the romantic. Before a dance at Christmas, "the Crystal Ball," my Dad bought a beautiful corsage for Mom. But he was afraid if he put the corsage in the fridge that his brothers would eat it, as a gag. So he took a steak out of the freezer and put the corsage on top of it to keep it cool while hiding it in his room. The corsage was sort of brown by the time Mom got it because he'd had it on the steak all afternoon, but it was the sentiment that counted. And my Mom still has that brown corsage.

Our whole family is very competitive. Easter-egg hunts can get pretty wild around the Lindros household. It's not as intense now, but it used to be like war. The Easter Bunny doesn't just throw Easter eggs all over the joint; she hides them in some tough spots. You've got to be very careful where you look. Brett used to leave his little basket out there and, when he wasn't looking, I'd be pilfering a few of his eggs. I'd leave mine out and he'd do the same. We always used to count up at the end to see who had the most. Mom would be the referee, Dad would help Robin look for eggs, and Brett and I would battle.

My parents have always put a heavy emphasis on school. My Mom spends hours with Robin, my Dad spends hours with Brett. Both of them spent hours with me. I would be struggling in school now if it weren't for all their help. And if we didn't have that closeness, I might have been more inclined to goof off in my studies. It was important to do well at school. When things weren't going so great in my classes, my Dad and Mom would talk about some of the pranks they pulled as students just to make me feel better. So, of course, I would follow suit, and either Carl or Bonnie would be busy the next day straightening things out with the teacher.

Math was my favorite subject. I could always do well in that. If my Mom didn't think I was being tested enough, then she would say, "Put him in advanced enriched," and she'd push for it. I remember once I flunked a Grade 9 English exam. I got 48 percent on it. My Dad was at the school the next morning. I was crying. I'd never flunked anything in my life. He spoke to the teacher about the difficulties I was having and found out what the problem was. I got a tutor. I ended up with a 78 overall. I don't know how I did it, but that's the way it went. You just don't accept failure.

My parents always stressed that whatever you do, you represent every one of us, so just make sure you do it right. Some people might think that's a heavy burden to carry, but I think it's helped me establish a real sense of pride in everything I do.

We've always had a lot of fun as a family. My Dad's a riot. He always kept things loose when we were out practicing in the backyard or when he ran scrimmages with some of my friends. There would be little competitions where you had to do push-ups if you lost. My dad wasn't exempt. To see Carl doing push-ups is like watching Garfield do push-ups—the two stubby paws and the gut hanging low. You would see his stomach just an inch off the ice. You would hoot, "Yeah, here we go, baby." He was just hilarious. I laugh so hard at some of the things he does.

One of his best stunts took place when I was ten years old, playing atom hockey for the Toronto Marlboros shortly after we moved from London. We were playing in a tournament in Ottawa between Christmas and New Year's. We had traveled there on our own team bus. I remember my Dad said to the team if we won the tournament he would clean all the outside windows on the bus—while barechested. We won the tournament. True to his word, Dad stripped down to the waist. It's minus-fourteen degrees outside and Carl's got his shirt off washing the windows of the bus. We could all see just fine on the way home—provided you could see through the ice that had formed on the side of the bus. He'd wash 'em, but he wouldn't scrape 'em.

Dad used to buy pucks upon pucks upon pucks for the backyard rink. But he also had other ways of keeping up his supply at the local shinny rinks, and he didn't care how he looked doing it. You've got to imagine this partner in a big chartered accounting firm climbing up a ladder to the top of the dressing rooms wearing this bulky parka and stuffing stray pucks into his coat.

Somebody would say, "Is that your Dad?"

"No, that's Carl."

I think one of the things I've learned from Dad is that there's a lot of stress in life. Deal with it, have fun with it, try to make it work. But when you play, play hard. His approach is, take it and go for it, but be thorough. If you're going to do it, do it well, but think about it first. There's no substitute for thinking. There's always a backup plan with him. There's got to be a backup plan. He's got more general knowledge than a lot of people. He's always trying to learn from people. That's what life is. It's learning from your mistakes and it's learning from your successes, but it's also learning from other people's mistakes and successes.

My Mom taught me not to take things lying down. Don't sit back. Words are one thing, and action's another. I discovered early that Mom was not one to hold her tongue. Bon doesn't like going on class trips, but I talked her into going to the zoo shortly after we moved to Toronto. My mom's from Chatham, a small town, very clean, no one litters. We're in Toronto now. Big city.

Big city kids. We're at the zoo. Kids start tossing out wrappers and littering. My Mom starts chewing them out. I'm whispering, "Mom, they're in my class, take it easy." She was not amused. "Well, they shouldn't be littering. The elephant will eat the paper and the whole colony will be gone."

Those who tried to give me a rough ride at the rink as a kid could expect to encounter Bon's wrath. When I was playing in the Esso Cup tournament as a thirteen-year-old, one of my former assistant coaches was trying to rattle me. I had switched over from the Marlboros to the Toronto Young Nats, and this assistant coach was still with the Marlboros. If I made a mistake, he would sarcastically yell, "Oh, Gretzky, too bad!" The other parents on my team were mad at him and one wanted to fight him in the stands, so the coach went off somewhere else to sit down.

Mom got wind of the situation, so she decided to settle the matter with him herself. The old seats at the North York Centennial Centre were double-seaters. She waited until this coach was sitting to watch one of the other games then jumped in right beside him on the same seat and wedged him right in. Bon looks right at him and says sweetly, "I hear you're comparing Eric to Wayne Gretzky. That's *sooo* nice of you." The guy didn't know what to do. He squirmed through the whole period, not saying a word. At the end of the period, he got up and got the heck out of there. My Mom looked over at his brother, who was sitting in the next seat, and said, "I don't think he'll be back for the rest of the game." His brother said, "Oh, sure he will." The coach never came back.

I can usually hear my Mom when I play. My Dad sits behind the glass at the far end. He's quiet at the rink; he just sucks it all in. Bon's up with all the other mothers. She is always saying "Skate." She just screams it—"Skate!" She would also yell, "You can do it!" Her encouragement was sure to give me a quick boost. When times are tough on the ice when you're a kid, you always need a little confidence. Sometimes you know inside you can do it, but you just have to be reminded in order to bring that inner confidence out.

Hockey's a very chauvinistic game. My mother knows a lot about it, and she speaks her mind sometimes. She's very firm about the values she believes in. I hear a lot of cracks about my Mom on the ice, but if Bon can handle it, I can handle it. And if my Dad can handle it, I can handle it. It's reached the point where I've heard every single word in the book. My Mom must be very, very busy, because I've lost count of the number of people who have told me they've slept with her. It doesn't get to me. If there's that much chauvinism and ignorance, that's fine. They can say what they want to say. It's not going to change my mother, and it's not going to change my feelings towards my mother.

Bonnie Lindros

It's really hard to watch some of the things that go on in junior hockey. When 4,500 people are cheering because your kid has just been speared and is curled up on the ice in pain, it really hurts. Hockey can bring some people right down to the raw basics. That's the way it is, and it's one of the reasons either Carl or I try to be at most of Eric's games. If there are thousands of people standing there booing and cursing you, you've got to know there are some people up there in the stands who don't feel the same way they do. There has to be somebody who cares.

When it comes to protecting the kids, I think mothers tend to do that more. I think it's a natural instinct—you just can't help yourself. It's always the mothers who get upset at the rink when things aren't right. When they see something that is totally dead wrong, they can't handle it.

Eric needs people around him whom he can trust, and who don't think of him as a commodity they can use but recognize him as a person who has limits. I always felt comfortable about his coaches with the Oshawa Generals, Rick Cornacchia and Larry Marson, because I knew they both cared about Eric as a person, not just as a hockey player.

Some fans in the opposition rinks are kind and positive, but it's hard for Eric to know that. In quite a few of the arenas, many people took the time to come up and say nice things about Eric. And we always let him know about it whenever we could, because these fans were certainly not the vocal ones at the arena.

Having my parents at my games means everything. It's a great feeling. They've been there for me all the way down the line. I started playing house league hockey before I was seven in London, and later played two seasons for the London Minor Hockey Association. We moved to Toronto when I was ten and I joined the Toronto Marlboro organization and played three years with them at the atom, peewee and minor peewee levels. Then I moved over to the Toronto Young Nats for two years, where I played minor peewee and bantam hockey, before joining the St. Michael's Junior B Buzzers when I was fifteen years old. My parents were always juggling things to make sure at least one of them was at my games. It would be tax season, and my Dad was buried under paperwork, but if there was an important game and it would be nice for him to be there, then he would be there. One thing was always made clear: the family comes first.

When I was playing in the Ontario Hockey League for Oshawa, I would always look for my parents during the national anthem. If their seats were vacant, I'd start wondering what had happened.

"O Canada . . ."
Did they have a problem with the car?

"Our home and native land . . ."
I don't think so. They've got a Volvo.

"True patriot love . . ."
They're very reliable cars. Or so they say.

"In all thy sons . . ."

Then they would arrive, and it's "Here they are, let's play." When I scored a big goal, I would usually look over there.

Sometimes, though, I don't know how my parents deal with some of the situations. It got really ugly last year when we played against the Sault Ste. Marie Greyhounds in the Ontario Hockey League final. I had refused to report to the Soo when they selected me first overall in the OHL draft two years earlier, because playing there would have made it impossible to finish high school and start university before I turned pro. Instead, I had gone off to Detroit to play Tier II Junior A hockey for the Compuware organization for half a season, and to finish my high school studies. Oshawa later worked out a big trade for my rights that wound up benefiting both teams, but the Soo fans never forgave me for not coming to play for their team.

My Dad came to every playoff game we had in the Soo to support me, and I really felt for him because of everything he had to put up with there. A lot of things were said that have no bearing on the game and don't even relate to what I did. To sit there through all the taunts hurled my way and the degrading signs plastered all over the building was really difficult for him. When we lost to Sault Ste. Marie, the first thing my Dad said to me was "I'm proud of you." We just lost and I hate losing, and my Dad hates losing. For him to say "I'm proud of you" really meant a lot.

Carl Lindros

Hockey for us has always been simply an opportunity to be together. I think we all got a lot of satisfaction from being out on the backyard rink. Working with the kids on their skills wasn't all that different than helping them with their homework.

The backyard rink and hockey became a focus for all of us, something we could share as a family. The thrust wasn't to try to make Eric or Brett a hockey player. The thrust was to have fun. The backyard rink looked like a carnival. We'd get the music going, we had the Christmas lights in the tree, and we'd just go out there and have a ball. Robin would often be out there gliding around on her figure skates and trying out a few new moves, while dodging the occasional puck.

It's quiet and relaxing to be outdoors on a winter night. It's sort of like fishing. There's not a whole lot that happens in fishing, but there's enough to take your mind off things.

Getting out on the rink is a good release after work, particularly when things are hectic. It was an interesting combination, because I enjoyed being outside and I was doing something with the kids. It was a win-win situation. I'm sure at times Bonnie thinks I'm nuts because of the amount of time I spend keeping that rink going, but it's fun.

Some families are into skiing. They buy all the equipment and go on weekend outings together for a big family gathering, a way to further strengthen those family bonds. For us, it was the same thing. Only in our case, the vehicle was hockey.

4

The Extra Mile

Rata-tat-tat-tat-tat-tat-tat! Rata-tat-tat-tat-tat-tat-tat!

The sound of jackhammers shook up our suburban Toronto neighborhood.

We had just moved to Toronto from London, and our new place had a huge backyard swimming pool. Not for long, though. It was a beautiful pool with clay and ceramic around the edges, but as far as the Lindros family is concerned, backyards are for rinks. The pool would have made it impossible to have a proper rink. So, naturally, the pool had to go.

Dad would be out in the backyard every day with the workmen, taking his turn on the jackhammer, drilling away at the concrete pool. It was in the heat of the summer in July, dusty and hot, and it was a brutal job. It took them nearly a week with two hammers going just to break up the concrete, and by the time they did, it looked like a bomb had hit our backyard. There were steel rods reinforcing the pool all the way through, and they had to take a blowtorch to burn off all this metal so that they could bust up the concrete. That pool would have been there for the next two hundred years.

Breaking up the pool was probably a breeze compared to filling in the gaping hole that was left in the ground. I think Dad must have started to wonder what he had got himself into, but there was no turning back. The hole had to be filled with sand, gravel and then dirt. That took about twenty truckloads of the stuff and another three weeks of evenings and weekends, with Carl and a helper giving those wheelbarrows a real workout. My Dad enjoys the physical work. He says he really enjoyed his summers working as a truck driver for a soft-drink company while he was going to university. He knew he'd be ready for football season after lugging all those cases of pop.

Still, we must have really had our new neighbors talking that summer. We turned a quiet, residential street into a construction zone. There were huge mounds of dirt on an orange tarp on our front lawn. Our neighbors couldn't figure out what my Dad was up to. They still wonder. But that's my Dad; he's his own person. I get mad at him sometimes, because occasionally he embarrasses me. But when I look at my friends I can see they get a blast out of him. All I can do is laugh. My Dad doesn't care what other people think.

A lot of people seem to find the story about the pool unique, but no one who knows our family was surprised by it. We were always doing crazy things. When my parents were looking for a house in Toronto, a rink was our top priority. They picked the area we would live in by putting a map on the bed with all the hockey arenas in Toronto marked on it. We wanted to be in a central location with access to as many rinks as possible.

You have to remember that my parents were both jocks, so they love hockey, too. They weren't doing it to turn their kids into professional hockey players; they were doing it to have something they could enjoy with their kids. There's a big difference. It was part of our lifestyle to do things like that. My Dad loves skating with his boys. My Mom says those are his happiest moments.

I wasn't too thrilled at first when my parents told us we were moving to Toronto. I was nervous, and I didn't want to make the move because all my friends were in London. But since I didn't have much say in the matter, I figured I'd better go along. I'm not sure how much say my parents had in it, either. For years, my Dad had been asked by his company to transfer to Toronto, but my parents, being small-town people at heart, had resisted the move. But, as Carl says, when you get the senior members of the firm suggesting you consider it, you have to consider it very carefully. So it quickly became "Toronto, here we come!"

I remember when my parents took us to Toronto to show us the house we were going to live in. On the trip home, they decided to cruise down Yonge Street so that we could see the downtown core. We were looking out the window, soaking it all in, when suddenly we saw this guy running up the street with a couple of policemen in hot pursuit.

"Mom, look, those guys have guns!"

"Carl, get out of here!"

It was a bank robbery. Brett and I started going nuts. There was a warning shot fired into the air. We thought it was great, because it was just like the movies. My parents were starting to worry about what they had got themselves into, but we were thinking, "Isn't this a great city? And that's not so far away from our house!" I decided Toronto might not be such a bad place after all.

The family was on a really tight budget after we moved to Toronto, but my parents always made sure their kids never did without when it came to activities we wanted to pursue. At the rinks, instead of buying pop, we brought our own juice boxes to drink after the game. But if we ever needed a hockey stick, it was no problem. If you needed tape, you got tape. My parents were always willing to scrimp a bit to make sure we were well supplied.

When it came to the backyard rink, my Dad would stop at nothing to keep it going through the winter. We'd have a thaw, and Carl's station wagon would make a beeline over to the local outdoor skating rink to load up on snow to patch the holes. They had a Zamboni attached to a tractor at the rink, and it would produce piles of snow. Dad would fill the station wagon with snow. We're not talking buckets here—he would fill the WHOLE wagon with snow. It would be all over the back seat. He was never civilized. The buckets were left at home, where they would be used to transport the snow from the car. You see, buckets would take up a little space.

The rink would turn into a summertime project, as well. As "Carl the Iceman" will tell you, the key to a good backyard rink is a perfectly flat lawn. He was always keeping a keen eye out for high spots. As soon as the ice started melting, he would tear out into the yard with his camera and start taking pictures. The areas that melted first were the high spots. When the summer came, Dad would be out in the backyard with his pictures trying to find the high spot again, and then he'd lift the sod to flatten it out. He says the work is good for taking some inches off his stomach— and he could use the help.

My Dad is not one for messing around. We have huge pylons that we use for our drills on the rink. A lot of hockey teams use those little orange pylons, but Carl's got the giant ones. My Mom called up the Department of Highways and asked if there were any used pylons we could have, and Dad drove right over to the warehouse to pick them up. He figures bigger pylons are going to better resemble a defenseman or another player. My brother bangs and smashes those pylons around so much, and it really ticks him off, because they just pop back up for more. That's the way my Dad is, though. He feels if you're going to spend the time and it's going to be fun, no sense dinking around with tiny pylons that are going to freeze up and crack. His attitude is, if you're going to do something, do it right.

My Mom's the same way. No obstacles are going to block her path if she wants to do something to help her kids. When someone tells my parents something can't be done, it just makes them that much more determined. When I was thirteen, I outgrew two pairs of skates and was in desperate need of a pair before hockey school started at the end of the summer. Finding a pair of skates that would last a whole season was always difficult. My Mom always bought skates that were about a size and a bit too large, hoping that my feet wouldn't outgrow them by year's end. When I was a kid, they'd stuff newspaper in the toes of my skates at the start of a season. The skates would eventually fit all right, and then they would get a little small, so my Dad would take a razor and chisel away at the insides.

The problem now was that I had outgrown all the conventional sizes, and the only answer was custom-built skates. Things looked pretty grim, since you had to book an appointment for a fitting at Bauer Skates months in advance, and there was no way I would have them in time for the hockey school. It looked like I'd be wearing socks with blades attached to the bottom.

Well, Bon wasn't going to give up that easily. She decided to phone the company one afternoon to explain the situation and see if they would help us out. The next thing we knew, Scott Walker at Bauer had agreed to give us an appointment in a couple of weeks' time, which meant the skates would be ready before hockey school started.

The story didn't end there, though. It turned out that they were sending the skates through the mail. On the Saturday before

I started hockey school, the skates still hadn't arrived, and we were getting more than a little worried. The people from Bauer were at a golf tournament and we tracked them down on the golf course to find out what had happened. They said the skates had been sent to a post office in Toronto and they told us which one. We roused someone at the post office, but he claimed the package wasn't there. We were at the cottage, so my Dad jumped in the car, drove the hour and a half to Toronto and started helping the attendant at the post office sort through the packages. The persistence paid off. The skates were there.

After my first day of hockey school, I called home right away to thank my parents and tell them about the skates. It was the first time my feet felt really relaxed in a pair of skates. It was like having faulty spark plugs in your car and then getting them fixed—everything just worked that much better. The difference was night and day. I said to my Mom, "We've got to get a pair of these skates for Dad. It's just like skating on clouds." I don't know how they did it, but my parents always came through. Bon and Carl were always willing to go the extra mile for their kids.

There were limits on hockey, though. We were never allowed to play summer hockey. We usually went to a hockey school for a week at the end of the summer just before the season started, but that was it. The basic rule about playing sports in the summer was, if you can get there on your bike, then you can do it. It was a time for my parents to relax, and they'd certainly earned it after chauffeuring us everywhere all winter. By the time school rolled around, you were just chomping at the bit to get your skates on again and play some hockey. I think it helped me keep my enthusiasm for the game.

My parents pretty much ran a shuttle service when I was playing hockey as a kid. I would be going from the backyard rink to the practice to the backyard rink to another practice. I just couldn't get enough of it. The rink was usually in full swing at least two weeks before Christmas, and I would be out there for two hours every weekday and at least six hours a day on weekends.

My Mom would bring out hot chocolate midway through. We'd always have lunch on the rink, usually sandwiches. You never threw any food on that rink; it was sacred. My brother used to put safety salt on the rink when he got mad at my Dad. I wouldn't talk to him for the rest of the day.

Brett and I devised a way to keep Mom on her toes when we were out there. We would take a sponge puck out with us, and Brett kept it inside his boot so it wouldn't freeze. Then, when Mom was looking out the big bay window in our kitchen, we would wing the puck right at her. It would bounce harmlessly off the glass, but Bon would have a bird.

Sometimes it was hard to find goalies for our practices. The husband of one of my Mom's best friends, Mr. Fowler, would come over to the backyard in Toronto every once in a while and let us fire rubber at him. He was about thirty-five years old and we would just be drilling pucks at him. I was about thirteen at the time, only a kid, but I could shoot a puck pretty hard. For the guy to stand there and take it earned my admiration. You would hear his gruff voice behind the mask every once in a while:

"Carl, you better have that beer cold!"

We had a goalie in Toronto who used to come over a lot, Raymond Saikkonen. We called him "the Rage." We played together with the Toronto Marlboros, and he was a great guy. His family was very straight, but they were really cool in their own way. Raymond wore his glasses when he played in goal, and he'd start sweating, and it would be so cold that his glasses would freeze over. He couldn't see a thing, but that didn't stop me from firing pucks at him. Ding! Right off his helmet. He would yell, "Hey, take it easy. I can't see!"

There was one big kid on that Marlboro team who used to pick on the Rage all the time. I remember I fought him at a practice

Above: Our first family portrait. I don't look too thrilled about it.

Left: Here I am at eight months. Check out the size of those hands and feet!

Bobbin' around. My parents got me my first pair of bobskates when I was one and a half. I loved skating right from the start.

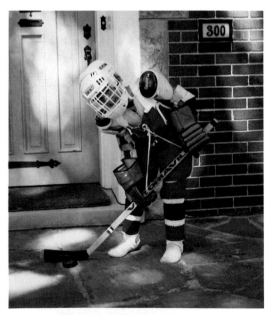

I got my first set of hockey equipment when I was six and a half. I used to wear it all day—even when I rode my bike.

My first hockey team in the Red Circle Minor Hockey Association in London. That's me in the second row, second from the right (with the ear-to-ear grin). The big guy in the middle of the back row is my father, Carl. He was one of our coaches.

Checking out a little table-hockey action with my cousin, Stuart Miller (left).

Making Christmas wishes with Brett and Robin. Mom's hand-made stockings hang in the background. I was eight at the time.

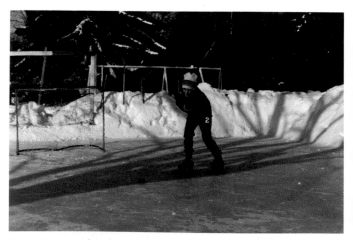

Practicing my slapshot on the backyard rink at our home in London, Ontario. I was out there every chance I got.

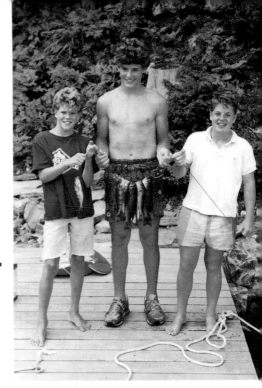

The big catch. Showing off the day's work with brother Brett (left) and friend Brian O'Hea (right) at the cottage. I still love to escape from everything by going fishing.

Relaxing by the pool—or what used to be a pool. We dug up the concrete pool at our Toronto home so we could have a back-yard rink. It turned out to be a real workout for my father. That's me on the right.

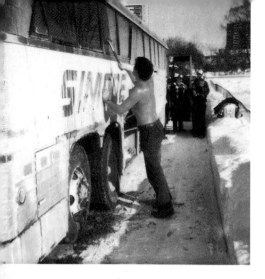

Chilled to the bone. My Dad promised to clean the windows while barechested if we won our atom hockey tournament in Ottawa. We won—and he cleaned. Did a fine job of it, too.

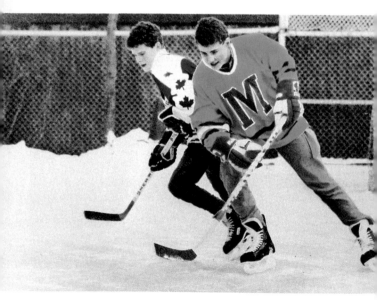

Getting a little practice in on the backyard rink in Toronto with brother Brett. I would spend hours out there—I had to be dragged in. (Photo by Jeff Goode, courtesy of *The Toronto Star*)

Looking pretty fresh-faced in my first go-round with the Canadian national junior team. It was three months after getting drafted by the Sault Ste. Marie Greyhounds. (Photo by *The London Free Press*)

Mom catches the action during one of my many hockey tournaments. I know I can always count on her support. (Photo by *The Toronto Sun*)

Meeting the press after my first game with the Oshawa Generals. My teammate Cory Banika is sporting a black eye.

Sharing a few laughs with my teammates during a break at the 1991 world juniors. Team sport is one of the greatest sensations. (Left to right: Felix Potvin, Trevor Kidd, Kent Manderville, myself, Chris Snell, and Dale Craigwell in the background) (Photo courtesy of Claus Anderson/ALLSPORT)

because he was taking advantage of the Rage. It was one thing to joke around with Rage, because Rage would joke around with you. But you couldn't take it too far, because Rage wouldn't do anything, and it would just hurt his feelings. I got smoked in that fight, but the Rage came up after and said, "Thanks a lot." I remember thinking it was pretty cool. If you don't have guts, you're not going anywhere.

Back in London, we would have friends over to the rink on a Saturday morning. Then Saturday night I would work on drills with Dad. But it didn't seem like work, it was fun. And if it had seemed like work, I don't think I ever would have done it. I'm just like everyone else. I don't mind working, but you don't work on something for six hours in a row, especially on a Saturday when you've got loads of free time. Saturday is God's gift to kids. It is *the* day for kids. I would skip the cartoons and be out on the rink. It was great. It was just me, my Dad and my brother. My Mom and sister would come out and we would have shooting competitions. One day we had balloons attached to the net, and you had to hit the balloon and pop it. Bon had a pretty good shot and she won her fair share.

We didn't always go out and just mess around on the rink. Dad would often have it set up so that no matter what you were doing—if you were standing still passing the puck or just flying around doing laps—it was for a reason. There was a purpose behind everything, even the stupidest drills. I mean, if you were tired and you just wanted to sit in front of the net and play baseball—you know, shoot the puck and bang it out of the air with your stick—then that would be working on deflections. There was always meaning behind it. There was fun there, and a way of making it beneficial.

We were always trying to wheedle a piece of ice somewhere. When we couldn't find any ice, we got a big piece of acrylic so that we could use it as a launching pad for pucks on dry land. In

51

Toronto, we set up a shooting gallery in our garage. The back of the garage is lined with mattresses so that we can put the welded net we had made in front and blast the pucks off the acrylic slab into the net. We use it mostly after the ice melts. At times, somebody will sit on a chair and drop pucks while the other person shoots. We'd do backhands, forehands, whatever we wanted to do. I would take buckets of pucks out there, plug the radio in and blast away. Dad would come out to talk to me while I took my shots. He would find some way of making it fun and challenging, by setting up targets or telling me to aim for a certain spot.

When we lived in London, I used to pester him to take me to work with him on the weekends so that I could shoot pucks in the underground parking garage at his office. I also used to shoot pucks in the basement at our home in London. The sounds would carry into our neighbor's basement, and for the longest time the Ralphs wondered where all that thumping was coming from. When we sold the house, the people who moved in had some questions of their own: they wanted to know why their basement walls were covered in black marks.

Once we started playing in leagues where bodychecking was allowed, Dad quickly made sure we were going to be able to handle ourselves. Mom went over to one of the local high schools and convinced them to lend us a tackling dummy. I think that was one of our favorite drills, taking a run at Carl while he held the dummy. We had a whole group of kids over one afternoon and we couldn't get enough of it. Dad used a lot of the same principles he learned in football, and it was really quite effective. Once in a while, Mom got to hold the dummy. Bon wasn't too fond of that, though. She also used to drop the puck when we practiced face-offs, but it got a little too nasty for her. She finally told us she wouldn't do it anymore if we were going to be so rough.

To help us better develop our passing skills, we had to use the straightest sticks, and we weren't too happy about that. The big stick when we were kids was the Cooper Mic Mac, because it had a wicked curve. I had the Artis, which was about as straight as they come. We would try to bend the stick on our skates to get a bit of a curve, but it would just fling back. Maybe that's why I learned to stickhandle better than anyone my age and learned the backhand flip pass, which is one of the greatest passes going. Not too many people can do it.

Dad and I had our disagreements at times out in the backyard. We'd get going on something like one-touch passes, and if Carl had trouble handling my passes that day, I would get frustrated, because there was only so much adjusting you could do. So I would start passing the pucks back to him real hard and then jump out of the way. He'd start laughing. I'd start laughing. It would be that much funnier, and we would stay out there that much longer.

It's funny looking back to the times when my Dad and I would take our sticks and pucks and sneak onto the rink at Victoria Park in London before it opened. It was a special time. There was a thrill to being on the ice when you weren't supposed to be there. Dad would always ask if I wanted to go, and I would nod with this big grin on my face. There's a certain part of you thinking, "This is bad. This is good." You couldn't shoot too far, because they didn't have boards and the puck would just go scooting off. It wasn't like our backyard Forum. You'd have to be very careful about your passes or you would be chasing that puck for a while. But just the fact that your Dad's out there messing around on the ice with you when you're not supposed to be out there made the whole time magic.

Carl Lindros

Bonnie and I tossed and turned in bed one night, but we couldn't get to sleep. We were with Eric at a little tournament in Amherst, New York, and for the first time it began to dawn on us that there could be something special there. Finally, after a few futile attempts at nodding off, we both sort of looked at each other at the same time, as if to say, "Did you see what I saw?" He was nine years old at the time, but he was starting to do things that made him stand out.

I guess it was the first time that Eric had caught up to some of the other kids who were excelling at that age. There was a player in Chicago who had matured a lot earlier and had more strength, and he had always been quite a bit ahead of Eric. But at this tournament, Eric had not only reached the level of this other player, he was surpassing him.

He had an understanding of the game. He would be doing something and you would scratch your head wondering what he was up to, but the puck would end up being there. He had an anticipation of the play, an ability to make lead passes that was beyond minor hockey. Minor hockey at that stage tended to be more along the lines of the better player grabbing the puck and going to the other end of the ice and scoring, but that wasn't what Eric was doing.

He also had willpower; if they were down a couple of goals, he would just buckle down. I guess it was a combination of drive, skill and mental aptitude. But it was the mental aptitude that struck me more than anything. I can remember, at the end of one period, he was going up the ice and he shot the puck from center ice. I was saying to myself, "Why the heck would you want to shoot from center ice? Who's going to score from there?" And then all of a sudden the buzzer went. Here was this young kid who was conscious of the time that was left on the clock. Nobody had taught him that. It wasn't anything the coach had said. He just knew.

Once we saw that Eric had an obvious love for the game, the next question was, "How do you make sure that this kid has the opportunity to take it as far as he can go with it?" You want to do it in a fashion that doesn't take the fun out of the whole activity. You can't analyze things to death, because then it becomes some sort of computer game. Sometimes the important thing isn't getting there, it's the fun, or what you learn along the way. It's a lot of hard work, but unless there's some enjoyment in it, then there's no sense doing it. You don't want things to get out of whack in terms of how important the objective is.

Bonnie was very good at identifying certain things that needed to be worked on. She tends to be more analytical in the sense of seeing the whole picture. And she spent countless hours organizing things for Eric, Brett and Robin and driving them everywhere. It's her energy that really pulls everything together.

We've also received a lot of gems of advice along the way. One fellow who was particularly helpful was Bob Vigars, who used to advise players on fitness training when I was on the football team at the University of Western Ontario. Bob had experience in working with young athletes and his track-and-field teams at Western have won a record fourteen national titles. One of the things I was interested in finding out from Bob was how they ensure that kids in sports like swimming, where they train for hours and hours, are well-balanced and don't get burned out and end up hating the sport further down the road. He said the burnout didn't come from hard work, that burnout very often came from a lack of positive reinforcement.

He used the example of Wayne Gretzky, because Gretzky was just emerging as a superstar at that point. Bob talked about the expectations that were placed on someone like Gretzky, who many people expected to score three goals in every game he played. He said if Gretzky is getting dumped on every time he scores one goal instead of three, then it won't take long for him to pack up his tent, because he won't have the drive to stick with it anymore. But if he's given recognition for things other than scoring, such as setting up other goals or stripping a player of the puck a couple of times, then it will be easier for him and others to keep everything in perspective. Gretzky will have the nights where he scores three goals and other nights where he'll score none, but Gretzky will always feel good about being Gretzky.

What he was saying was, don't let the expectations become unrealistic. You have to have expectations, but they should be reasonable ones that you can strive for and that you're likely to achieve. It's when they become unrealistic that the athlete burns out.

The other key part of the advice we got from Bob was that kids who are involved at the high end of sport lead a very structured life. In Bob's mind, it is important to have a time during the year when there's very little structure. It doesn't make a lot of sense to play a top-end, organized sport like hockey and then move into something like baseball at a very competitive level. He said if you really want to excel at a sport, it is important that there be times when you do other things that are totally different and of a different structure. So our kids have never been involved in summer hockey or any other organized sport. They do some skating in August to get ready for the season, but that's it.

Another person we sought counsel from was Bobby Orr's father, Doug. We went to Parry Sound one day on a camping trip and we just knocked on his door. Being the friendly individual he is, Doug ushered us right in. He said he had heard about Eric through some friends, and he took us downstairs to show us some of Bobby's many trophies. We chatted for a while, and his main message to us was, "Keep your kid a kid." He said, "If he's as good as I think he is, the hockey will all fall into place." He seemed to feel that maybe Bobby had been cheated out of some of his childhood by joining the professional ranks so young. We listened very carefully and really took that to heart. We spoke a few times after that. In fact, it was on Doug's advice that we eventually wound up asking Rick Curran to handle Eric's business affairs. Doug jokes with Rick every once in a while, asking when he's going to get his commission.

I think what we've attempted to do as a family is to think ahead and try to plan for the future. I don't think it should ever be construed that we're wizards at this. I don't think we did anything different than a lot of other parents who try to give their kids some guidance, hoping they'll get into a certain university or that they'll marry the right kind of guy or girl.

There was lot of satisfaction in working with the kids on their skills in the backyard. It's not that I was that proficient as a hockey player, but there were some coaching ideas I saw in other sports that stuck with me and that I thought could help the kids in getting more enjoyment out of the game. I think the level of coaching now in hockey has changed dramatically from when I played. At that time, I thought the coaches I had in basketball and football had a better way of teaching things. In basketball, when they taught you how to do something like a lay-up, it was broken down into ten steps, whereas in a typical hockey practice they would say "Go in and shoot." They weren't talking about which foot you're shooting off, how you hold your stick, whether your eyes are up or not, what you should be looking at when you move in on a goalie, whether you should shoot high or low or wherever.

In basketball, you'd be forced to do lay-ups with your right hand *and* with your left hand. You would dribble as much with your left hand as you'd dribble with your right. In hockey, we always tend to shoot on the forehand, and most players, even a lot of players in the NHL, aren't that proficient with their backhand. They always take the puck from the backhand and move it to their forehand before they shoot. If you can use that backhand, it's an extra weapon in your arsenal. Gretzky is an example of a player who is just as dangerous on his backhand, and it's obvious from books about him and watching him that it's an asset he acquired through practice and hard work.

Most players, when they see someone use a new skill, get a lot of fun out of learning it and making progress with it. On the other hand, if you just throw the puck out all the time and play shinny—and there's certainly a time for that—you tend to use the skills that you're already good at. But if you break down a skill, and players start to recognize that they can improve on it through hard work over a period of time, then they're going to make the effort.

When the kids were moving from non-contact hockey to contact hockey, I realized, from having played football, that you could use a lot of the same principles to teach them about hitting. It just gets back to the idea of fundamentals in terms of balance, extending your knees, how to use your shoulders and keeping your head up—basic stuff. It was just taking something that you spent hours and hours doing on a football field and saying, "Let's take a few hours and apply it to the hockey situation." The kids loved it. Most kids are gung ho and they want to be macho, but they're also apprehensive, because they know that if you don't do it right you can hurt yourself.

It's a matter of control. Your objective isn't necessarily to absolutely kayo the other person; the idea is to make sure that other person doesn't get by. I can recall one afternoon we had about half a dozen kids in the backyard. Some were Brett's age; some were Eric's age. They were all getting their licks in. We would start with the dummy on a stationary basis, then show them how to bodycheck someone in open ice or hit somebody straight up. We didn't do it much beyond three-quarters speed, because otherwise I'd have been knocked for a loop.

In football, you spend a lot of time doing neck exercises, and the kids should be doing the same thing in hockey to help protect themselves. At the end of most of our practices outside, Eric would usually do some isometric exercises, just like we did in football. It's something that's seldom done, yet it's something that anyone can do at home.

My dedication to keeping the backyard rink going certainly made me the butt of a lot of jokes. They'd laugh at me because I would be out there at all hours of the night, either flooding it with the sprinkler or trying to patch it up with some snow. When you spend a lot of hours working on the rink, there's sort of an attachment there. When it melts, it symbolizes the passing of another year. You can always tell spring is approaching, because the rink gets shorter and shorter. Last year, when the ice got pretty bad, Brett would venture out on it at night wearing golf shoes so that he had some stability and could shoot pucks. It worked out well.

On the night of our final skate, the kids would usually take their sticks and crack the ice up and throw chunks all around. Brett would typically threaten that he was going to go into the house to get some salt to throw on it to make sure that it melted. But sometimes the cold weather would return for a short spell, and everybody would be chuckling because I would be out there late one night trying to get the rink going again. It was hard for me to accept the end of a season.

Looking back on it, I think there are two sides to the success Eric has enjoyed so far. He's been fortunate in that he has been blessed with a certain amount of natural athletic talent, but the other part of it is that he has worked hard to develop his skills. You do have to work hard, because things seldom come easy.

Sometimes, being blessed with a skill can be a detriment. For example, as a student, you might do very well at high school because you're very bright, but you might not develop good work habits, and by the time you get to university you can get blown out of the water.

The same thing can happen in sports. Perhaps, as a young person, you might be bigger than the rest of the kids, so you don't work on things such as stickhandling. As you try to take the next step up the ladder, you might get left behind because you can't keep pace anymore. There has to be a balance there. Just because you've got certain skills, they won't necessarily get you where you want to go.

It gets back to the whole idea of catching the kids when they're doing something right and building on it. Just from my own experience as a hockey player, I know what a vital ingredient confidence can be. I remember what Paul Terbenche told me when we were both in the Chicago farm system trying to make the Blackhawks. He was a smaller player with good skills who would go on to play in the NHL for a while. I was a big guy, but I always felt gawky and uncoordinated.

Terbenche said to me, "I really wish I had your size. You can do anything you want out there." I was kind of taken aback by that. I said, "What do you mean?" He said, "Your biggest problem is self-confidence. If you go out there and think you can do it, you can do it. Just go out on the ice and think you're the best player on the ice." I did that for a couple of weeks, and I was amazed at how well it worked. I quickly became a starter. It was a simple point that he made, but it really showed me, when I was dealing with the kids, how important it is to make sure there is that sense of confidence. You don't want them to be cocky, but for a lot of kids there's a tendency for them not to realize how good they are. You improve by building; you don't develop by destroying.

Bonnie Lindros

Carl is always trying to learn new things, and I think our whole family is like that. We don't sit back and act complacent. We always keep moving; we never sit and rest. We're always thinking, "How can we get better? How can our kids do better?" Luckily, we've made a lot of good friends who have helped us along the way. Carl is the type of person who doesn't do that much talking because he's too busy trying to figure out what he can learn from you. We make a good team, because he'll think of something and then I'll do the legwork to get it done.

As soon as Eric started to emerge in hockey, we started renting some extra ice time and organizing things a little bit differently so that he got the opportunity to develop his skills fully. We never felt threatened by his talent. Eric is certainly a lot better at hockey than Carl ever was, but that never worried Carl.

Bob Vanderaa came up with the idea of renting the arena in nearby Dorchester for an hour when Eric and Bob's son Mark were playing together back in London. All the defensemen from the team would go out there, and Carl and Bob would work with them. Carl would read all the instruction books and he knew how to run an excellent practice. He's really into the teaching aspect. He likes to look at the big picture, but not too much escapes his notice. He can even can tell you how wide a certain player's skates are.

It was always important to us that our kids feel good about themselves. I was impressed by the way my friend Wendy Ebers dealt with her kids. She always made a point of introducing them to you. The minute you walked into her house she'd say, "Now here's Matt and Bethy, come and say hi to Mrs. Lindros." It was different from when I was a kid, when the general philosophy was that children should be seen and not heard. Her kids were brought into the center. They didn't hang around for hours, but they were always made to feel a part of things. And they had a lot of confidence. I recognized that and followed her example. The kids were always introduced and treated like individuals. I think that gave Eric a lot of self-assurance.

When we had Christmas parties in London, I would dress the kids up in matching pajamas, which I had sewn. Their job was to greet the guests. They looked like cute little bugs running around and taking the coats upstairs. It gave them a chance to meet all the people at the party, and I think those little things gave them more confidence.

But I must admit, some days Eric got me down, and I could get very angry with him. I probably said things that weren't as boosting to his self-esteem as they could have been. But he did drive you to the wall!

My parents always kept things fun, but managed to make them challenging at the same time. I found that I was always yearning to reach that next level. When we used to drive to the rink before a game, we would talk about things I could concentrate on developing that day. We would usually pick three things. It was an opportunity for me to get better as a hockey player, as opposed to just concentrating on winning or scoring. It wasn't a heavy-duty thing; it was something I really enjoyed. The other thing that was typically said was, "Have fun." After the game, they would compliment me and say, "Hey, that went really well today!"

Mom and Dad both really understand the game. When you get into the playoffs, where the little things can make the difference between whether you advance or not, Carl is just like a player—he becomes more intense and focused. Because you play the other team in as many as seven games, he starts to zero in on their weaknesses and how you can counter them.

He was at his coaching best when we played Kitchener in the Ontario Hockey League finals in 1990, the year that we won the Memorial Cup for Oshawa. We were one game away from losing the series, down three games to one, and Mark Montanari was doing a great job shadowing me and keeping me off the scoreboard. My Dad started calling up all his sources, asking them for some tips on how I could break loose and whether they had spotted any weaknesses in Kitchener goalie Mike Torchia.

Before the start of the next game in Oshawa, my Dad took me out to the parking lot at the Civic Auditorium to fill me in on what he had learned. You've got to picture this scene. Everyone's standing there lined up for tickets, and we're out in the parking lot with hockey sticks, and Carl's about to give me a few tips. I was trying to hide between the cars.

"All right, Dad. Let's do it."

He went through everything. He didn't care what it looked like; if it was going to help us win, he was going to do it. He didn't tell me anything extraordinary. It was just little things, like how to fare better on the draws, but those small things can make the difference in the heat of the playoffs. Maybe the most important message of all that was communicated was "We believe in you." My Dad didn't even have to say it—I felt it. And that gave me the confidence to go out there and make it happen.

Not all the things Carl showed me were within the rules, because the opposition seemed to be bending them in the way they were playing against me. You do what you can to win. You're a survivor. The winner prevails. I don't claim to be an angel. I get sticked all the time, I get hit illegally and I do it back. There's a time and a place. What goes around, comes around. Live by the sword, die by the sword. Montanari started cutting me with the sword. He died by the sword.

Over the course of the last three games, I gained confidence and I shot Montanari down. During the game that started for me in the parking lot, I had two goals. The next game we went back to Kitchener, and they were set to wrap it up on their home pond, but we won again, and I had a hat trick. In the seventh game, in Oshawa, I had another goal and we beat them again to win the series. I had six goals in the last three games, and I attribute that to the help that my Dad gave me.

My Mom knows what's going on, too. You can't pull a fast one on her. If I'm not skating hard, she's the first one to yell at me. She tends to see some things in a different way than my Dad does. Bon's good at seeing how the players react to certain situations, what's going on between the coach and the players, what's going on between the two coaches. She notices that at a certain point in the game certain coaches will have their players start checking you differently—things most people would never think about.

She knows about the mental side of the game, too. During the Kitchener series, one Ranger fan had a megaphone and used it all night long to shout sarcastic comments at our team, and I was his favorite target. He was so obnoxious and loud that it was hard at times to tune him out. My Mom realized what this fan was trying to do and asked our friend Lynn Vanderaa to rent a megaphone to bring to the next game to cheer the Generals on. Every time the Ranger fan started blasting away on his megaphone, Lynn cranked it up to drown him out. The Kitchener players soon began to refer to Lynn as "the bitch with the megaphone." But she accomplished what my Mom had hoped—she stopped this fan's attempts to get us off our game.

Bon also knows exactly what the ref's thinking. If the ref's not too good socially, she can point that out to me. When a ref isn't very good socially, you don't talk to him. You say "Yes, sir" or "No, sir." If a ref is more social, you talk to him more, it's more open. Let's face it, you try to use all the ploys you know.

Hockey is like a book. Within the book, there are sections. And within the sections, there are subsections or chapters. And within each chapter, it's sort of like a paragraph where there's an opening statement, three things you talk about and then a closing statement. It's like an essay. If you can break everything down, it makes it that much easier. I can break it down.

If I have the chance to see someone demonstrate a skill a couple of times, I can usually break it down and go out and work on it in the backyard. It's got to be in your head. I analyze it, trying to think what the person doing the skill was thinking. If he's got his head down when he's making a stop, you have to watch where his eyes are. Just little things. Some people stop and have their heads down for a reason. It's sort of a fake that they're lost, but they keep on going and they know exactly where everyone is. You've just got to take the skill apart bit by bit and throw it back into your style using your own crazy-glue.

I would watch someone in practice who was really slick with the puck, like Dale Craigwell while I was with Oshawa. He could cruise in and make the moves on the defense even at the end of practice when the ice was really chipped up. I would need perfect ice, perfect stick, perfect everything just to get by a stupid pylon, so I would look at how Dale did it, and I would be out there in the backyard going over it with my Dad or my brother, making the dekes on those pylons. That's how you learn.

I've also got to be in the right mood, kind of relaxed, to work on a new skill. If I'm mad about something, then I'm in a shooting mood. I just shoot the puck as hard as I can. I never try working on a new skill right before a game. I usually try something mid-week, presuming the games are Sunday or the next Friday. I practice the skill a number of different ways on the rink so that it represents each possible situation. I try things like making backhand chip passes to the pylons, over and over and over again. People used to think I was nuts, making all these passes to pylons. But I try to picture someone like Robbie Pearson, my linemate with the Generals, or Jarri Kurri, moving in to take the pass.

I think I first decided I really wanted to be a professional hockey player when I was fourteen years old. I looked at all the options and thought my best chance for success might lie in hockey. I was having fun, it was a competitive game, and I was good at it.

Mark Messier of the Edmonton Oilers was the big guy for me. I was impressed by his physical presence and his leadership qualities—and also his Porsche. I didn't really have a favorite team. I always liked winners, and I was on and off the bandwagon all the time. Watching hockey games on TV wasn't a big thing for me; I would rather be playing than watching. I'm a doer, not a spectator.

It all comes down to a willingness to learn and work hard. Those are things that were instilled in me by my parents. They've always put their kids ahead of everything else, and I hope someday to be in a position to do a lot of things for them and the whole family. My parents have never been to England, and my Mom has always dreamed about going there. They're going to go to England some day. I've got more to pay back than I'll ever earn—money doesn't even come close to it. You just can't put a price tag on it.

5

Welcome to the Real World

I can pinpoint the exact day, hour and minute when hockey stopped being just a game for me. Something of the feeling I had on the backyard rink was lost forever when one of the men in suits, sitting at their big round tables at North York Centennial Centre, stood up to make a declaration.

"The Sault Ste. Marie Greyhounds pick Eric Lindros."

The 1989 Ontario Hockey League draft was underway on a hot Saturday morning, May 27, but as far as I was concerned my season was already over. For that matter, I figured my hopes of a pro career were also gone forever. Whatever the future held, this much was certain: hockey would never be quite the same for me again.

It was clear well before the draft that Sault Ste. Marie wanted to pick me first overall—and my family and I had made it just as clear that I had no intention of playing there. I had recently turned sixteen, and I just didn't feel ready to live nearly five hundred miles away from home. We're a close-knit family, and that support is very important to me. From the meetings we'd had with the people from the Soo, there was also no doubt that my education would suffer because of the team's heavy travel schedule. My parents wanted me to get some university courses under my belt before I started pro hockey—something that would be impossible if I were playing in Sault Ste. Marie. The hockey experts were predicting I'd be playing in the NHL at age eighteen. That left only two years to get my high school diploma. At the time, I was still in Grade 10 with a few extra credits from summer school. I was just a kid; I didn't even have a driver's licence yet.

Under the rules of major junior hockey, I had no say in the matter; the Ontario Hockey League officials hold all the power. If you want to play in the OHL, they expect you to go to any team that drafts you, no matter how far away from home it may be or what your feelings are. So you have some players as young as fifteen selected in the OHL Priority Selection draft having no control at all over where they end up. The OHL rules have been challenged in court—as far as the Ontario Supreme Court by one hockey player's family—without success. The Supreme Court judge who heard the case said young hockey players should not be "dealt with as commercial commodities or a side of beef," but he still decided in favor of the league, because he didn't want to interfere with the "internal rules and regulations of clubs."

I was honest about the situation with Sault Ste. Marie. I could have lied and told the Soo that I was packing my bags and going off to college, or that I was going to stay in Junior B for another year, but I didn't. I was upfront, but, as I would learn later, some people don't respect you for that.

Before the draft we met with the people from Sault Ste. Marie—including Phil Esposito, then one of the owners of the team—and tried to explain our feelings about the situation. They said they understood and we got the impression that they were going to work something out, probably by trading my rights. But the night before the draft, it became obvious that they had no intention of trading me at all. There was money to be made from my name, and it looked to me as though they weren't about to squander the opportunity.

The Sault Ste. Marie franchise was in financial trouble at the time, and the owners were negotiating to sell the team. One offer, we later learned, came from the Compuware organization in Detroit, which offered $600,000 for the franchise on May 17. I guess Esposito decided that the team would be worth more with me on it, so he went ahead and drafted me. Compuware later upped its bid to $1 million, but the team stayed in the Soo, because the city itself and local investors stepped in to match the offer. Because the team had drafted me, Esposito and his partners sold their interest in the club for what I thought was a much better price than they otherwise could have.

The whole episode showed me that hockey is a bottom-line business, even at the junior level. I felt like a piece of meat. Hockey had been a game to me until then. When I was playing Junior B for St. Mike's a year earlier, they kept talking about how the organization was having financial problems and that they might not have a team next season, because we weren't drawing a lot of people to our games. That didn't affect me, because I never thought of hockey in financial terms. I was thinking, "Hockey is a game, it's for fun." But all that changed on the day of the OHL draft.

I was devastated when the Soo drafted me; it was so disillusioning. All I wanted to do was play, and they were making it so hard for me. I remember sitting in the kitchen, thinking my hockey career was over. Where was I going to play? Paul Henry, a scout with the Canadian Olympic team, came over that afternoon to offer me a chance to join them, but I felt I was too young to go out to live at their training base in Calgary. I could have done it, I could have managed, but I wouldn't have been happy.

My parents were really slammed in the press over the whole issue, particularly in Sault Ste. Marie. It really upset me when one reporter from the only daily newspaper in the Soo started writing all this negative stuff about my mother, and how she was interfering with the way things should go for a junior hockey player. He sensationalized everything, and there was nothing we could do about it.

I was told by some people before the draft that everything would be taken care of and it would work out fine, but things were not okay until my parents stepped in and *made* things okay. Then everyone started criticizing my parents for interfering, when all they were doing was trying to help me out, to get me in the position I wanted to be in. They did what any parents who care about their kid would do. Nearly two years later, a radio reporter from the Soo, after a lengthy interview with my Mom, finally concluded, "You mean you were lookin' out for your own." At least one person in the Soo understood.

Carl Lindros

The whole affair had so many twists and turns that it took a real emotional toll on Eric. There was a lot of stress and a lot of pain for a sixteen-year-old to deal with. He started having spontaneous nosebleeds a couple of weeks before the draft, and he wasn't getting much sleep. On the eve of the draft, when he heard the Soo was going to select him the following day, he sat by himself in our backyard and his nose began pouring blood. He spent most of the next morning crying in his room. In fact, we all stayed in our rooms; there wasn't a dry eye in the house.

I felt that the Soo owners played around with a kid's life for their own financial gain and, to me, that was the most disturbing thing. I'm sure, in Phil Esposito's mind, junior hockey is a business, and drafting Eric made good sense from his perspective. But it seemed to me that no one ever really took Eric's feelings into account. We had a very emotional conversation on the phone with Phil Esposito the night before the draft. There was a series of phone calls that evening, from ten o'clock until two in the morning, and we really thought that Phil was going to reconsider his position. I still recall walking into the draft about an hour after Eric had been selected. There were all these junior hockey officials sitting there like the Knights of the Round Table, determining the immediate futures of all the available kids. I went up to the Sault Ste. Marie table and exchanged a few words with Phil. I was almost ready to pop him one, but that would only have made things worse. I just thought the whole thing stank.

People said we were snubbing the Soo, but we would have made the same decision regarding about two-thirds of the other teams in the league. We were looking for basically three things in a team: that it be located in a community with a university; that it be within a two-hour drive of home; and that the organization place a strong emphasis on education. There were about half a dozen teams that were a good fit. We would also have said no to Windsor, which is close to our hometown of Chatham, and to Ottawa, and a number of other different places. It wasn't just the Soo or the North.

We felt it was very important that Eric be exposed to university before turning pro. Since that wasn't going to be possible in

71

the Soo, there was no question in Eric's mind that he had to play somewhere else. When we met with the people from the Soo—Esposito, coach Ted Nolan and part-owner Angelo Bumbacco—they brought their education consultant. As the meeting went on, the consultant came out and said it would be difficult for Eric to complete high school, let alone get exposed to university, in a two-year period. Once that was established, there was no sense in talking about how nice the people in the city were or what could be done to minimize the travel.

To us, stressing education was a way of helping Eric build his self-esteem and become a more well-rounded person who sees there are other options in life. While you're at school, you see how other people live and think, and it also takes you out of the locker room and helps in developing your social skills.

We wanted to be within two hours of where Eric was so that we would be there for support when he needed us. It would have been hard to travel to a place like the Soo regularly, particularly when you have other children. You can't be devoting the whole weekend to one kid and ignoring the rest. In Eric's case, that desire to be close to him was even more important, because we knew there was going to be a lot of media attention and high expectations, and whenever there are high expectations you end up with a lot of ups and downs. I think family is really important when someone is hitting a low, because they can help you bounce back.

The thing that was really frustrating was the way we were portrayed in the Soo newspaper. We gave numerous interviews over the telephone because we thought if people understood our rationale they might accept our stand. For several weeks we read the Soo newspaper in the local library, and we were disappointed. We were being painted as elitist—big city versus little town. It really bothered us, especially since both Bonnie and I are small-town Chatham people at heart. Most of us aren't perfect, but I don't think we like to be slammed without cause.

Bonnie, in particular, became a target for one of the Soo reporters. I think he chose her because she caught him cornering Eric behind a van in the parking lot on draft day. Eric had asked us to take him to the arena after lunch, because he wanted to have the fun of watching some of his friends get drafted. Instead of approaching Eric in the arena, this reporter waited until he went to the car to get his camera and then corralled him outside and shoved a tape recorder in his face. Bonnie didn't feel this was an appropriate way for an adult to approach a sixteen-year-old kid, peppering him with questions on such a controversial issue, and she really let this reporter know it. Shortly after that, he started doing a serious hatchet job on her in his newspaper.

It got so bad that Bonnie's former classmates who were from the Soo wouldn't even speak to her at their twenty-year reunion. They read in the newspapers that the Lindroses didn't think the Soo was good enough for their son, so you could understand why they might have felt that way.

There were also a number of people who felt that to play in the OHL was an honor and nobody should challenge it. I think that's an issue that parents and league officials should look at more carefully. While the needs of most new recruits are considered by the league, it just wasn't going to work out in Eric's case. It's not that much different from graduating from high school and deciding what university or college to attend—you want to go where you think you'll fit best. Because you've got a desire to have some parity within the league, it's understandable that you just can't throw the draft wide open, but there's got to be a degree of give and take—there's no doubt of that in my mind.

Bonnie Lindros

There was never any discussion about the possibility of going to the Soo after the draft; Eric knew playing there wouldn't work for him. The OHL had its set of rules. Rather than challenge them, we just decided it wasn't going to work for us. We never dreamt they would wind up changing the rules.

Carl and I had come up with a number of alternative plans, so we moved on. The University of Michigan was a possible option, since we had all visited the campus a few months earlier and met with former NHLer Red Berenson and his coaching staff. But Eric would not be eligible to enter university for almost a year, so he needed a place to play in the meantime. Red Berenson had given us the phone number of Andy Weidenbach, the coach of the Detroit-based Compuware team that played in the Tier II league. We called Andy and left a message on his answering machine, and he called us back within ten minutes. In the meantime, Andy had already phoned Jimmy Rutherford, the head of Compuware's hockey operations, because he wasn't sure what he should do.

"Eric Lindros's family has phoned to see about him playing for me," Andy said.

"Well, phone them back," said Jimmy.

"But we've already got a full roster," Andy reminded him.

"Oh no we don't," Jimmy countered.

Jimmy Rutherford, realizing Eric would only be there until January, decided to expand the lineup for him. Eric felt better almost immediately—he now had a team and something to focus on.

Eric had to decide for himself where his priorities were, and his priorities were with school. When he was growing up, we always talked about how, with education, it would be easier to make your own life decisions and life choices. Eric recognized that right from the start, and he worked hard at school. He didn't always do it because he loved it, but he is a person who feels he has to do his best at whatever he does.

Not many kids would have done what he did that summer. He finished his high school exams in Toronto on a Friday afternoon, and he was in a new school in a new city in a new country on Monday morning. He had signed up for summer school in Detroit, because he was fast-tracking through the system so that he could finish his high school by January 1990 and be ready to start university more than a year before he would be entering the pros.

The people at the Compuware organization in Detroit were just great to us. There were about five lawyers and staff who met Eric at the door when we arrived. It overwhelmed us because, after all the grief we had been through with the OHL, we now had somebody trying to help us make it work. It was certainly a striking difference. Eric ended up at Bloomfield Hills Andover High School for the summer, and the fellow at the guidance department was terrific. He helped us arrange the proper courses so Eric could graduate in January.

Eric went to a different high school in the fall, in Farmington, Michigan. We didn't tell them Eric played hockey because we wanted to keep everything low-key. The only person who knew was the principal—until Eric's picture appeared on the cover of *The Hockey News* with the headline "Whiz Kid: Meet A 16-year-old Destined To Be An NHL Superstar." They just about died. Unlike Canadians, Americans like to parade their heroes. They hung the article on the principal's wall and in the halls of the school.

Everything worked out much better than we had expected, and the kids in the States were great. The coaching staff at Compuware taught Eric a lot. But perhaps the best thing about the whole experience was that he boarded with the Vellucci family in Farmington. The Vellucis and their next door neighbors, the Mac-Dougalls, really looked after him and treated him just like one of their kids. I remember Judy Vellucci asking me what Eric's favorite foods were, and I said "Everything—and lots of it." She soon found out that I wasn't kidding.

Judy Vellucci
(Eric's billet, Farmington, Michigan)

I had been hearing about this kid for months—the word was out about him—but I thought his name was "Lynn Dross." The move to Farmington was a tense situation for both Eric and his family, because they had no idea what he was coming into. I saw it as a great opportunity to meet someone special, and I wanted to make his life with us as normal as possible. I was strongly aware that this might be the last bit of normalcy he'd ever have. The people in Michigan didn't know him yet; the people in Canada were just learning about him.

It seemed at times he was down on humanity, just sort of discouraged that people would do the things that they do. He's very sensitive. People would never think that anyone that big and strong would have so much heart, so much sensitivity, but he does. He loves his sister and brother, truly adores his parents, and he's a very grateful young man. But I think the experience with the OHL draft changed him a lot. That was the real world. What I think he learned was that when it comes right down to it, your parents have your best interests at heart and nobody else does. Everybody else wants a piece of you. He was so young to have learned that. And it was like he put on emotional armor in response.

The first day Eric came to Detroit he was scared to death, but I didn't realize that. We live out in Farmington, which is a nice little middle-class suburb where you don't have to lock the doors all the time. All my kids were off golfing because it was a nice, hot summer day, and I figured I had better go to the grocery store because I heard he ate a lot. I said, "Eric, make yourself comfortable, put your clothes away, I'll be back in a little while."

I guess because of all the things he had heard about Detroit, and being in a new place, he was really frightened to be left alone in the house. As soon as I went out, he went upstairs and locked himself in the bathroom. He later told me he was up there flushing the toilet and counting the tiles to take his mind off his fear. He was a nervous wreck. When I came home, he was sitting at the top of the steps, his eyes scared like a rabbit's, because he had no idea who was walking through the door. His concerns didn't end there, though. For the longest time I couldn't find my big paring knife, until I was cleaning in Eric's room one day and found it under his mattress. He was really afraid.

As a family, we wanted to get to know Eric the person, not Eric the hockey player. That was how we focused on him. He doesn't act like he's anything special; he's unpretentious and unassuming. There are so many people who are far less talented who are so cocky. He was so different, and we really learned to love him. He's just a great kid.

Bonnie had warned me about his appetite. Luckily, because I have a large family, I was semi-prepared, but he could still pack it away like no one I have ever seen. I was buying pounds and pounds of lunch meat and tons of tuna fish. He could eat a six-pound can of peanut butter in three weeks, and his idea of a slice of watermelon was a quarter of the melon. One time he came home from school at two-thirty in the afternoon after having five sandwiches for lunch, and it smelled like he was baking cookies in the oven. But it was actually the toaster going full tilt, because he was toasting and devouring a whole loaf of raisin bread as a snack.

My kids would cut him up about his appetite all the time. One night, I left a great big piece of steak on the kitchen counter to defrost because I was thinking of making a beef burgundy. But I always told Eric, "Whatever's there is yours, just go get it," and he took me at my word on this occasion. I came home and he had cooked the steak on the grill and wolfed down the whole thing. "I hope you don't mind," he said, a bit sheepishly. I got a real kick out of that, because it could have fed a whole family. Unfortunately, he ate it before his game and was sick at the rink.

The only area where Eric fell short was in keeping his room clean. I don't think he ever hung up any of his clothes in the six months he stayed with us. He just left them all in piles on the floor. When *Sports Illustrated* came out to do an article on him, he kept it pretty quiet because he didn't want to sound like he was boasting, and he didn't tell me until two days before they came. I told him that maybe he should clean his room just in case they wanted to take some pictures in there. No response. I said to him, "Eric, I think it would be a good idea." It was the only time he ever got mad. He just said, "If they don't like me the way I am, that's their problem." I couldn't argue with that. He's a great student, a great hockey player, a great kid—let him have his room messy if he wants.

When the photographer from *Sports Illustrated* came, he said, "What about Eric's room, can we take some pictures?" Eric was behind him, shaking his head to signal "no." My son Mark, trying to cover for him, said they could use his room instead. Unfortunately, they had to pass Eric's room to get to Mark's room. As they're going past, Eric slowly pulled the door shut. The photographer knew something was in there and peeked inside. I heard them all howling.

As far as the hockey went, Eric looked like a man among these little boys when he was out on the ice for Compuware. I know the coach, Andy Weidenbach, was thrilled to have him, but it was obvious he was too good for the league. You could tell there were times when he could have been flying with the puck but he was passing it to his linemates instead. He was always thinking of their feelings, which I'm sure harmed him at times. But he didn't see it that way, because his goal was to fit in with the other kids. He's willing to set himself apart with his discipline and his goals, but I don't think he wants the outside world to set him apart.

OTHER VOICES:

Andy Weidenbach (head coach, Compuware)

Eric was really conscious that he didn't want to be singled out and get any special treatment; he wanted to be one of the guys. He did whatever it took to help the team, whether it was killing penalties or playing a defensive role or whatever we needed. There was no question that he was just too much for the other teams to handle. When he wanted to go, he could. One game in Detroit, he really turned it on and had six goals and four assists.

The opposition quickly learned not to get him agitated. One time we were playing in Fraser, Michigan, against the Junior Red

Wings, and they were all trying to harass Eric by grabbing him, banging him, sticking him. All of a sudden we saw one of the Red Wings lying flat on the ice. Eric had got tired of this guy jabbing him with his stick and he knocked him out cold with a right hand—all while Eric still had his glove on, and the guy was wearing a full wire cage. The referee never saw it. They stopped the game with a minute left in the period and decided to resurface the ice, because the guy was stretched out and they had to revive him. He was seeing stars as they dragged him off the ice.

Even then, Eric was really living in a fishbowl. All eyes were on him, scrutinizing everything he did, and I was amazed at how he handled it. The media came to all the practices and all the games; never a day went by that somebody wasn't at the arena. He tried to downplay it and get some of the other guys involved. The media used to ask him, "Are you a Gretzky? Are you a Lemieux? Or are you more like Messier?" He wasn't comfortable with that. I think he's different from Lemieux and Gretzky and Messier, but he's got a little bit of all those players in him. He's got the good reach and hands of a Lemieux, he sees the ice like a Gretzky, and he's tough like a Messier. When the press asked him those questions, Eric always used to say "I'm a Lindros." I guess that's really the best way to describe him, because he really is his own person.

I'll never forget Eric's performance in the exhibition game we played in early September against the Windsor Spitfires of the OHL. The rest of the teams we played weren't close to the size and toughness of the Spitfire team. We were playing up a level, being a Tier II team, but you would never have known it. Eric was so fired up for that game, because of what had happened with the OHL draft, that he singlehandedly took on the whole Spitfire team. He scored two goals and two assists, and he was delivering hit after hit. When the Spitfires tried to get tough because they were losing and they were frustrated, Eric just started manhandling guys all over the ice. I wouldn't say he had the entire Spitfire team intimidated, but he certainly stood up to them. Nobody on that team could handle him. That's when I knew this guy was special. He wasn't afraid of anything. I've never see any one player do what he did that night—*ever*—and I've been coaching for fourteen years. We whipped them 8-0, and Eric was a one-man show, no question about it. It was a sellout crowd, and they were certainly impressed. Most fans walked away talking to themselves.

I had a mission that night against the Spitfires. The way I looked at it, the Spitfires represented the OHL, and I represented my side of the story. I was the plaintiff; they were the defendant. I was my own lawyer; the Spitfires were the OHL's lawyer. I had to prove to the judge, jury and the defendant that I was right. It was my one chance to show them that they needed me in the league. You only get so many opportunities, and that was one I wasn't about to squander.

A few months later, on November 13, the OHL Board of Governors changed its rule regarding the trading of first-round draft picks. Teams had to wait a year before trading their first-round picks previously, but now they were allowed to deal them from January 1 to January 10 of each season, giving Sault Ste. Marie the opportunity to trade me, something they wouldn't have had the chance to do under the previous regulations. A lot of people dubbed it "the Lindros Rule," and my family and I took a lot of flak again. But they didn't change the rule just to help me; they changed it to benefit themselves. In me, they saw a potential drawing card and a chance to make a lot of money. If the opportunity to cash in on my name and reputation hadn't been there, that rule would never have been changed.

The experience in Detroit made me mature quickly. It's different when your Mom's not there to take care of everything for you. I think I gained a lot of independence while I was there, and it helped me get used to living away from home.

The Velluccis were great; they really made me feel at home. They're such a tight family unit. They have a softball team they sponsor every year, Vellucci Incorporated. The whole family plays on the team, and they all have the name Vellucci printed across their backs. There was always something going on.

I experienced "Devil's Night" for the first time with the Velluccis. Devil's Night, the night before Hallowe'en, is a great time for pranks, and Mark Vellucci and I made sure we took full advantage of the occasion. We decided to decorate the house of their next-door neighbors, a fun-loving bunch called the Mac-Dougalls. We went up on their roof and wrapped their house in toilet paper, from the weather vane at one end to the TV antenna at the other. The MacDougalls thought there were bears on their roof when they heard our footsteps—Mark, at six-foot-five and 230 pounds, was bigger than me by about an inch and a couple of pounds. The MacDougalls got their revenge, though, by wrapping my Jeep in toilet paper at Christmas time. We always had a lot of fun. It was a nice change, because it was so far removed from the Sault Ste. Marie fiasco.

Throughout my stay in Detroit, there was a lot of speculation about where I might end up in the Ontario Hockey League. After the rule about trading first-round draft picks was changed, seven teams were reportedly trying to strike a deal with Sault Ste. Marie for my rights. I finally learned my destination just before leaving for the World Junior Championships in Finland with the national team: I had been traded to the Oshawa Generals, the same junior team Bobby Orr once played for. I knew the deal was done the night the junior team was playing in Belleville, Ontario, but I couldn't say anything because it hadn't yet been announced publicly. I had never seen the Oshawa Generals play before and I didn't even know what their uniforms looked like, but at least it was close to home. Sault Ste. Marie would wind up getting a hefty package in return: three players, two top draft choices and $80,000 cash right away, and another two players in the form of "future considerations" over the next two years. Greyhounds general manager Sherry Bassin figures the deal—which included NHL draft money they later picked up— was worth $500,000 to his team. The press called it "the biggest trade in junior hockey history."

After finishing up at school in Detroit following the World Junior Championships in January, it was off to Oshawa to finally get my shot in the OHL. I was a little apprehensive about how I would be accepted by the team. The guys on the Generals were pretty good right from day one, but still, I had to prove myself to the boys, and one night in Belleville I was presented with my chance.

I was out on a line with Dale Craigwell late in the game against the Belleville Bulls. We both had two goals, and our coach, Rick Cornacchia, had sent us out there to give us a chance at a hat trick. Well, some of the Belleville players started slinging racial slurs at Dale, who is black, and they were trying to start a fight with him. I grabbed the player who was going after Dale, and Scott Boston of Belleville grabbed me. The three of us were tangled together. I told Boston, "I don't need to fight you. We're going to get suspended. There's no sense." He obviously didn't agree—he punched me in the face. I just lost it. I started pummeling Boston until the referee mercifully stepped in to pull me off him, and a huge brawl erupted. Boston wasn't in very good shape afterwards. A few minutes after he left the ice, an announcement came over the loudspeaker:

"Would the team doctor please report to the Belleville dressing room."

The boys spent a lot of time watching the replay of the game video on the bus ride home, and I think they realized then that I was more than willing to stick up for my teammates when the need arose.

Bill Armstrong and Iain Fraser, two of the veterans on the team, really looked after me that first year in Oshawa. I was young, I was aggressive and I was crazy in some ways. I did some things I wouldn't normally have done as a rookie, but I didn't care. The other teams all knew that if they hit me, they would have to deal with Bill Armstrong. "Army" used to wear this black mouthguard, and he was the meanest-looking guy I've ever seen. He was crazy, but he's the guy you want on your team. Iain Fraser didn't fight that much, but he didn't need to, because he was the captain and had the opposition's respect. Somebody would start up with me and "Fraz" would come along and say, "Leave him alone. Just let him play—because he'll kick your butt!"

Team sport is one of the best sensations in the world. No matter how hard things get or how down you feel, there are always people out there who understand. And those people who understand are your teammates. There are certain things that take place in the dressing room, that take place on the road, that take place on the bench—and that's right where they stay. We tell each other everything. Everything. We know all the dirt about each other, and there are certain things guys are trusting you not to tell anyone else. Certain things take place during the year, good and bad, but it's all part of being on a team, and we all grow with it. The coach might ream a couple of players out, but no one goes out and tells the reporters about it.

It's the same thing if one of your teammates gets into a scrap and doesn't fare so well. The next shift, someone goes out there, and if he's fighting, he's not fighting just for himself, he's fighting for redemption. It's like he's representing his family.

That Oshawa team was so confident, so cocky—we felt we were the best club in Canadian junior hockey, and we were determined to prove it. We ended up in the 1990 Memorial Cup championship game against our OHL rivals, the Kitchener Rangers. The game went into double-overtime, but we always knew we would win. We just knew it was going to happen. I remember Cory Banika sitting at the end of the bench saying, "Will you guys hurry up and score here because I'm getting a little bored with this game." He was serious. That's the kind of guy he was, a real character, but someone who came to play every game.

It was Billy Armstrong who came through for us, though. He'd had only two goals the entire season, but he turned sniper in that second overtime when he sailed a shot towards the Kitchener net and it deflected past goalie Mike Torchia. I felt sorry for Mike, even though he had stoned me the whole series. We're buddies; we played on the same team one year when we were kids and he's been on my backyard rink many times. But on the ice, if I get a chance to run him, I'm running him. And when I'm in front of the net, he's slashing my legs and giving me the blocker to the back of the head. Once the game's over, though, it's "C'mon Taco, let's go grab something to eat."

We won because our so-called third line—Dale Craigwell, Cory Banika and Joe Busillo—was better than any other third line in the nation. None of those guys got above sixty-five points during the year, but they came through whenever we needed them.

I played on a line with Mike Craig and Iain Fraser, and we had a good series. Craiger and Fraser were scoring; I wasn't scoring, but I was setting them up. I played hard and I worked hard and I wanted to win so badly. While I didn't play quite as well as I had hoped, I was still one of the top point-getters in the tournament, with nine assists. But because I didn't score a goal, the critics automatically presumed I didn't play well and fired a few darts in my direction. If I had scored four goals, they would have been saying I was great, or that I was a puck-hog. But we won, and that's what counts.

There was a bit of *déjà vu* for a couple of my teammates at the end. Mike Craig got hurt and was replaced on our line by Brent Grieve. Iain Fraser and Grieve had played together on the same line for most of their lives and had always dreamed about winning the Cup while working as linemates. It was a great experience for them, and I was really proud to be part of that line.

All in all, it was a great ending to a difficult season. Finally, the hassles involving the Sault Ste. Marie fiasco seemed far away—I didn't know they were far from over.

* * *

"Woooo! Woooo! Who's coming with me!"

I went flying out of the dressing room and jumped out onto the ice at the Sault Memorial Gardens. It was game three of the 1991 Ontario Hockey League finals, and the Sault Ste. Marie Greyhound fans finally had what they wanted—a chance to abuse me in person. Nearly five thousand people were packed into the rink; they probably could have filled the place three times over. Another three hundred were jammed into the Elks' Hall next door to watch a closed-circuit telecast of the game. The hooting and the boos echoed throughout the arena. I was pumped. I rode the red line at center ice to get the adrenaline going. Riding the red line is something I often do in the warm-up to get myself psyched. I cross into the other team's zone a few times, as if to send them a message. When they come into your arena, it's like, "This is my barn, this is my territory, this is Generals' ice. I'm a General. I'm a big part of this team. This is a big part of my ice. So watch out!"

There was so much hype leading up to the game; everything was blown out of proportion all over again, just as it had been when I said I wouldn't report to the Soo nearly two years earlier. The people in the Soo had promised to give me a rough ride, and the pre-game build-up had reached such a fervor that extra policemen were stationed all over the rink. We also had a couple of security guards staying with the team full-time. It's kind of bizarre when you have to take those kinds of safety measures at a junior hockey game because of fears that some loon might get out of control, but I don't think it really affected me. The way I viewed the situation, it was just like having a whole bunch of babysitters there—and I wasn't the baby.

The fans were hanging over the glass during the warm-up, taunting me. Every time I dumped the puck into our zone, I sent it right their way. Thwack! The puck would bounce off the plexi-glass. Then all the soothers would be tossed onto the ice. There were more soothers on the ice than you see at a nursery, and I'm pretty sure I saw a few of the adults who threw them take them right out of their own mouths.

The warm-up went really well, with all but three of my shots going into the net. I felt calm, poised, very sure of myself. I looked at the games in the Soo as more or less a proving ground, a place to make a statement for myself that I'm not evil, I don't wear black, I'm not the made-up, superficial jerk they're so proud to portray me as in the papers, or talk about on the radio. I'm just a regular person using the methods my parents brought me up with, and using their morals and values.

I was proud of the way I played in the Soo, but we never really got on track as a team. The Greyhounds won games three and four to go up three games to one in the series. Going back to Oshawa, I still felt we could win the series and advance to the Memorial Cup again. There was no way I was going to quit. Even when you're down, you just have to keep plugging away and playing honestly.

I think you brand yourself when you're a kid as to whether you're a winner, a follower or an "I don't care." When you're a winner, you try to take as many followers as you can with you and try to change as many "I don't care"s into followers. I feel that I branded myself a winner. I had a hard time playing with kids my age because I was so competitive. When people talked about me, I wanted them to say, "He plays for such and such a team. They've got a winning team and a lot of really good players." I liked that attitude. There's nothing better than being associated with the best in a winning atmosphere.

This past season in Oshawa, we didn't have quite as much depth and we lacked toughness, both mentally and physically. As the series against the Soo wore on, the Greyhounds seemed to want the victory more than we did. We were winning on talent that season, not because we were playing well. You can't win on talent throughout the whole playoffs. We would put together one or two good games, then we would lose, and then we would come back and win a game on sheer talent, a game that we should have lost. So then we would get it in our minds that we could play on talent alone and win. But you can't beat a team like Sault Ste. Marie on talent; you've got to beat them on guts, desire and a never-say-die attitude.

We beat the Greyhounds back on our home ice in Oshawa to narrow the series to three games to two, but then they clinched the title back in Sault Ste. Marie. Most of our players were crying in the dressing room afterwards. We were all hurt because we personally felt we had the better team. But certain spokes on our wheel fell sick and certain spokes on their wheel turned into two spokes, and they rolled right over us. People were telling us to keep our heads up. But how can you keep your head up when you're second best? We had a pretty good year, collected 100 points and had the best team on the road, but we just couldn't put it together for the last series.

We all tried hard, but that doesn't mean we tried as hard as we could have. There were things we could have done differently.

I don't think you can say "I tried my hardest." There's no such thing, because there's always a lot more that you can give.

I'm scared of defeat; I can't handle it. I don't like any aspect of it. It's meaningless unless we win. It's just a game, and I know that, but it means so much. I pride myself on being a winner, on being in a winning atmosphere and always being the best I can possibly be.

The Soo fans made sure to rub it in every chance they got. The first night I played there, I didn't think it was so bad. It was more a matter of people taking pride in their own city than because of something that they felt I had done wrong. I found it interesting and I don't think you would see it in a lot of cities. But after that, it all took on a different tone. They would keep chanting "Eric Who? Eric Who?" and never let up, even when they were winning the last game by a large margin. When the Soo's Colin Miller scored a goal, it was announced on the loudspeaker as "Sault Ste. Marie goal scored by *our* No. 88, Colin Miller!" It was all so petty.

Of course, there were long lines of fans waiting for autographs after games, many of whom I'm sure cursed me every time I was within shouting distance. One night I was standing there signing autographs and, after I signed something for this one boy, he spit on me and told me to "F——off." He looked to be about nine years old.

There were a lot of signs directed at my Mom, and I heard about her all game from the fans. Who needs that stuff? Dump on me if you have to, I made the decision. But the decision's made, it's two years old. Get a life! I'm still bitter about the whole scene. It was over, the trade was done. Oshawa got what they wanted. Sault Ste. Marie got what they wanted—they beat Oshawa in the finals and earned a trip to the Memorial Cup—and the fans there still had to carry on. They just couldn't let it die; they had to dwell on it and sensationalize everything. I guess the people from the Soo need more experience in winning gracefully. They never thought beyond their hockey team. What I did was best for me, and most of them couldn't understand that. They never really understood the whole situation.

There were some people in the Soo who were really decent to me. Some came up and said, "You did what you had to do and I hope you're happy." I really appreciated that. It's too bad more of their neighbors didn't have the same insight.

I was tired of junior hockey in a lot of respects at the end of the Soo series, but I still wanted to play. Getting knocked out of the playoffs left a sour aftertaste. As long as the puck was still being dropped, I wanted to be out there.

My life revolves around hockey right now. Ending the year on a losing note doesn't do much for your summer. There are always questions in the back of your mind: "Why?" "What went wrong?" "What could we have done differently?" You might still think you have the best team, but you can't prove it. You're done. Branded winners want to win. I hate losing.

6

Growing Pains

The constant blare of the trumpet reverberating through the house would have tested anyone's nerves, especially since the same jarring mistake could be heard over and over and over again.

When I started music class, Mom was kind of hoping I would get a soft and mellow instrument, like a clarinet, so she was a bit concerned when I came home carrying a trumpet in a big suitcase.

"The teacher told me I had trumpet lips," I said, and Bon wasn't about to argue with that.

I liked playing the trumpet, but I really hated lugging it home from school, and the daily grind of practicing was a drag sometimes.

On this particular day, the noise was also starting to grate on my Mom. She could hear my trumpet blasting away upstairs and she began to tire of hearing me continually misfire on the same notes. So Bon finally decided to head upstairs to check it out, much to my dismay. She quickly discovered that the repeated mistakes were no coincidence—she had been listening to a tape recording playing over and over. There I was, stretched out on my bed relaxing, while a recording of my trumpet practice whirred madly on a tape player strategically placed at the top of the stairway. My cover was blown. Trumpet practice was never as much fun after that.

I eventually worked my way up to lead trumpet in the school band, but I soon found that music and hockey weren't going to mix. In Grade 6, I was heading to the big annual peewee hockey tournament in Quebec for the first time, which directly coincided with the Kiwanis Music Festival our band had entered. We didn't realize the two clashed at first, and when I had to tell my music teacher, Mr. Manning, that I would be missing the festival because of my hockey commitment, he was just fuming. He gave me a lecture on where he felt my responsibilities lay.

"Eric, I want you to get your priorities straight," Mr. Manning declared.

"I think they are straight, Mr. Manning."

I went to the hockey tournament and was quickly replaced as the lead trumpet. I was still a member of the band, though, and the following year my competitive nature got the better of me. We were performing at a big concert and I was sitting right beside the new lead trumpet, Jenny Wheatcroft, one of my music lesson partners. It was only fair that Jenny take over as lead, but I was still really peeved at being bounced, so I began whispering some words of encouragement to her.

"Jen, you're going to screw up. Jen, you're going to screw up."

By the time Jen's big solo came around, she was pretty rattled. And Jen screwed up. Royally. Bon really blasted me on the way home when she'd found out what I'd done, but I thought it was pretty hilarious at the time.

My musical career came to a halt at the end of Grade 9 at North Toronto Collegiate Institute. My teacher told me I could no longer play in the band because I was going to miss some practices as a result of hockey. Although I had an A+ in music that year, I was left with no choice but to drop the class.

As a kid, I was just as competitive in school as I was on the ice, because I wanted to get good marks. I had a pretty heated rivalry going with this girl named Stephanie. Whatever we did, we were totally caught up in trying to beat each other. The big thing in school at the end of the year was to win the citizenship award. I won it three years in a row on the boys' side, while she accomplished the same on the girls' side. But neither of us won it the fourth year, because we both went totally overboard in our attempts to outdo each other.

I really got into cross-country running in Grade 4 at Ryerson Public School back in London. The Board of Education organized a lot of races that year, and we Ryerson Rebels tried to make sure we entered every one. It was not a good sport for kids with big joints, and I was often in a lot of pain, but that wasn't going to stop someone who hated losing the way I did. I improved with every race leading up to the city championships. There were about five hundred kids jammed together at the starting line for the championships and, because the starting gun wasn't working properly, they used a whistle to signal the start. The whistle sounded and I took off like a rocket and moved out in front. The only problem was that it was a false start, and I was so focused that I didn't hear the weak toots of the whistle trying to call me back. I ran about a kilometre before they finally caught up with me, and then the race had to be restarted. I wound up seventeenth overall, which was pretty good all things considered, but it was pretty upsetting. That was the end of my cross-country running career.

All that running nearly short-circuited my days as a hockey player. Because we were always training on concrete, I ended up with a condition called Osgood-Schlatter, a knee problem that afflicts growing kids. The pain persisted, and I eventually went to a sports clinic, where they had some special braces made for me. The braces are made from the material used for wet suits and have pads in the knees. I still use the braces every game; they've become part of my uniform.

I scrapped more than I should have during my school days, but there was nothing like a good fight to secure your rung on the ladder. When I was in kindergarten, I got into a fight with a kid who was in Grade 3. The Grade 3s and 4s always had the big football games going, and it looked like a lot of fun, so I wanted to be part of it. But there was always one guy who thought he was the king of the playground, and he wouldn't let me join. I wanted to play so badly that I fought the guy. We went at it outside the school by the big green garbage cans, and I scored a unanimous decision. His mother phoned our house to give Bonnie an earful.

"Do you realize your boy has beat up on my son? He's got cuts and bruises all over."

When the lady found out I was in kindergarten, she was so embarrassed that she hung up the phone.

Still, I've always done well in school. It wasn't that I studied that hard; it was more a matter of making sure I did all my work. School's not difficult, unless you don't pay any attention to what's going on in your class. If you do listen and you're still having problems, then it's time to ask questions. People are so worried about how they look and acting cool in school that they forget why they're there. I never wore great clothes or did anything special, because I wasn't out to impress anyone. I just went to class, listened and had fun with it.

My parents always said, if you're not keeping up in school, then you can't play hockey. As a result, I'd have to sacrifice shooting the puck in the garage for homework on many occasions. I was expected to maintain an 80 percent average, which I knew I could do if I just concentrated on my work. If I ever had a problem, I would go to my parents. My Dad would help me out with some of the math stuff; my Mom would look over my English to make sure it was okay. I had a pretty heavy load—eight subjects—at North Toronto Collegiate Institute, so I usually tried to do my homework at lunch because I had Junior B hockey practice every afternoon.

I felt like an outsider at high school. Because I was so busy with hockey, I was considered to be some dumb jock. I had a few friends there, but I didn't go to any of the dances or formals because I never really had a girlfriend. It didn't really bother me, because I was into hockey. The way I looked at it, I was dating hockey.

The fact that I was going through incredible growth spurts at the time—I grew about nine inches in one year—didn't make me feel any more comfortable. I felt uncoordinated and was always tumbling down the stairs in school. Nothing ever worked the same way twice. One time I put my arm straight through a plate-glass door at school because I missed hitting the panel on the side when I went to open it.

I just wished that it would stop, that I would reach my height. When it came to hockey, I prayed I wouldn't grow right before the playoffs or a big game. It would really affect my skating and my shot. My shot was never the same twice. I'd use the same action, the same flex on my stick and everything else, but it would always be off by a little bit. It was like continually adjusting the sights on a rifle, gauging and regauging the scope each time you fire a shot.

As far as sleep went, there weren't enough hours in the day. I was always tired. One day I went to bed at nine at night and got up the following afternoon at two o'clock. Some people say too much sleep isn't good for you, but I've still got to have those big-time siestas. If I don't get ten and a half hours, I'm in trouble. My favorite thing is to do nothing but sleep.

I never showered when I practiced with the Junior B team at St. Mike's, because I hadn't matured physically yet. I would put my street clothes back on and head for home. The guys on the team would kind of joke about me. I rode to practices back then on my Mom's old blue bike, which had this big wicker basket attached, and the boys at St. Mike's got a kick out of that, too. Angelo Libertucci, the goalie, called it the ugliest bike he had ever seen. Angelo and Dino Grassi taped it up one time, put pucks in the spokes and hung it on the wall in the dressing room. It was pretty funny.

The bike at least had one more wheel than my previous mode of transportation. I got a unicycle for Christmas when I was twelve. I loved the challenge of something like that and, after practicing downstairs by balancing with my hands on the ceiling, I could ride it within an hour. It was a lot of fun. I rode it to school, but I felt really self-conscious on it. Then one day a van came through the neighborhood and stole all the kids' bikes at the school. My parents offered to replace the unicycle, but I didn't want to get another one because it made me look so different from the other kids.

The only time I really felt part of my high school was in my math classes in Grades 9 and 10. We had the greatest teacher, Mrs. Kathy Love. The thing I liked best about her class was that it was a team effort. If you showed up and you tried really hard, then you were guaranteed to pass. When she did something on the board, only two students might know how to do it at the start, but by the end of the period everyone had learned it because we worked together as a group and helped each other.

It was very social because we talked all the time, but we were always talking about math. If we did really well and we had some time off after homework check, we'd pool our money and one person would sneak out the window to go to the variety store to load up on Freezees for everyone. We had to keep it quiet, though, because the head of the math department caught us on a few occasions and would start yelling at Mrs. Love. But she would say, "Look at their work. Would you come in and look? I am teaching here. They're having fun."

Most of us were in different classes after Grade 9, but we all transferred back into Mrs. Love's class because we enjoyed it so much. I didn't know too many students at the school, so I looked forward to period nine math because we had a great bunch of people—we were a real team.

I took a full load of classes every year and usually went to summer school, but it all paid off because I completed high school far ahead of schedule and now have two courses to my credit at York University in Toronto. Sooner or later, I'm going to get my university degree. I'm not sure when, but I'll get it.

What Randy Gregg did really impresses me. To complete his studies to become a doctor while playing defense for the Edmonton Oilers is amazing, especially when you consider the pace of a pro hockey life—daily practices, team meetings, games and a hectic travel schedule. And then toss in what it would take to establish a career in medicine—the studies, all the reading, working as an intern at a hospital. It's hard to believe that someone could juggle both, but he wanted to do more with his life than just play hockey. He's not only a high-calibre athlete, he's *Doctor Randy Gregg*.

In junior hockey, I think a lot of players get caught up in the fact that they're big celebrities in a small town, and they start to believe their life is set and they don't have to take school that seriously. Some guys take courses like basket-weaving or underwater door-slamming. Craig Donaldson, who was on the Oshawa Generals the first year I played there, worked really hard at school, got all his credits, did very well in calculus and went on to play hockey at the University of Western Ontario. He's someone who had his mind set in the right groove.

Hockey has always been a way for me to get away from everything. If I've got problems with a university professor, problems with my friends, problems with my car . . . I can forget about that on the ice. When I'm on the rink, it's my time. If you want to talk to me, don't call me off the ice. It bothers me when people try to pull you away from something you love just because they're in a hurry. If they'd have the courtesy to wait a little bit, then everything would work out fine. It's just that it's my time, and no one's going to take it away from me. It's just like some people love their sleep—don't take their sleep away from them. It's like that with me at the rink—don't touch my ice.

I get psyched for practices. Let's face it, practice can be routine and sometimes guys just don't want to be out there. I have a lot of fun at practice and I look on it as my role to make sure my teammates are having some fun too. If you can keep things light, then it doesn't become drudgery and guys end up working even harder.

When I was in Oshawa, we'd always be playing practical jokes on each other. Our repertoire included taping sticks together, putting tape on the bottom of skate blades, covering doorknobs with Vaseline, and nailing someone's shoes to a bench. I hid my linemate Robbie Pearson's false tooth in his jar of hair gel once. He wasn't too thrilled with that, because it darkened it and hurt his image as a ladies' man. But he would always make sure to exact his revenge. Whenever the team went for meals, you could usually count on Robbie's false teeth ending up in someone else's glass before we left the restaurant.

Some of the funniest things happened on the team bus. You log a lot of mileage on the road in junior hockey, and that's where much of the team bonding takes place. There's kind of a pecking order on the bus. The coaches and assistant coaches sit up front, followed by the management and business people and reporters, and then it's the rookies, second-year players and so on. I had a great seat in my second year with the Generals, third row from the back. Robbie Pearson was behind me, Dale Craigwell was in front of me and Paul O'Hagan and Jean Paul Davis were at the back. Mark Deazeley, a friend of mine from high school, sat a few rows in front of me, and he was often the pranksters' target.

We had so many wild guys on that team, and there was always something happening. It was the best time. You can't replace those moments. One of the big things to do when we were bored was to pick on Deazeley. It would usually start off with someone firing some jujubes in Deazeley's direction. It was sort of funny, because his seat was directly behind one of the TV screens. Sometimes, "the Deaz" would bang his head on it if he turned really quickly and jumped up. Clunk! So he'd start firing the jujubes back. Then the food was passed out after the game. It was usually Swiss Chalet chicken. So a bun would go flying, followed by pistachio nuts, then a bone. It finally built up to the point where Deazeley would turn around, grab his container of barbecue sauce and a half-chicken and just drill the whole thing at the back of the bus. Then everything erupted. It was a major food fight. That would happen all the time. It was hilarious. I liked the security of being in the dark on the bus. You could get away with some stupid, crazy, immature things and have a blast doing it. Later, you would look at it and think that was really dumb, but it was a great release.

Deazeley was a great guy, because you could always joke around with him and he never took it that seriously. One of the promotions we had in Oshawa was that any fan who got a puck in the stands during the game won a free submarine sandwich. We stacked a case of pucks in Deazeley's dressing-room stall to make it look as if he was stealing them to collect some free subs. He was always worried about his weight and we kept bugging him about it. So Deazeley would arrive at his stall and one of the guys would say, "What are you doing here, Deaz? Are you going to go to the sub shop with all these? Hey, coach . . ."

Another stunt I enjoyed was moving people's cars after we came home from road trips. It would be freezing cold in the middle of winter, and guys usually started warming up their engines before they went into the rink to unpack their equipment. When they came out, they often found themselves walking a little farther than they planned, because their cars were hidden on the other side of the parking lot. We had a lot of fun, but we were careful never to go too far with our jokes.

The nice thing about the end of a hockey season is that it usually means it's time to open the cottage. My parents built the place bit by bit with a lot of sweat and toil over the years. It seemed that whenever we drove up there we always had our station wagon stuffed with building materials. Our cottage is nothing extravagant, but it's our place to escape from it all. The summer is time for a little "R and R"—Rockin' and Rollin'.

I love sitting in the cottage and listening to the radio. We have this old AM-FM radio and eight-track player that our Grandfather Blake gave us when he moved out of his home. My brother broke the eight-track so we wouldn't have to hear Mom play "'Ol' Blue Eyes" one more time. It's kind of beat up and we only get one AM station where they play the same songs every thirty minutes, but I just crank it up and let loose with a few howls. I turn up the radio full blast in the car all the time and just shout out the words. I find it's a good release.

The cottage is a great place for the whole family to get together. My cousins have a place right next to us, and our grandparents often come for a visit. They hold these parties called "Moonlight Madness" in the area, and at times we've had all three generations—my parents, grandparents and the kids—partying together there. That's what I enjoy most.

Things have always been kept low-key in the summer. Up until this past year, most of the people at the cottage didn't even know I played hockey. One of my Mom's friends there found out for the first time when she saw us in a documentary on the television show *W5*.

Fishing is one of my favorite pastimes up there. I like being seduced by the environment. I'm not going to change the environment; it's going to change me. It's just being out there and trolling along and relaxing.

My friend Scott Bailey and I have fished together since we were seven. Worms were expensive when we were kids, so, being kind of cheap, we would try to dig up our own. We also made sure we had the thickest lines possible for fishing because we were afraid of snagging something and losing a lure, which meant we would have to buy another one. I'm sure the fish could see our lines a mile away, because we used fifty-pound test. We thought we were going to catch Moby Dick, but were always happy to settle for a little sunfish or bass.

I used to read all the fishing books and study the various techniques. There was an expert fisherman I watched on TV all the time, and one summer he visited our bay to fish for bass. I went out to see him because I read his manuals and thought he was a real hotshot, but he hooked his lure on the dock. I lost some respect for the guy. What kind of an expert hooks his lure on the dock?

Scott and I had a lot of fun fishing; there was no competition. We'd just sit out there in the sun and tan, and have a few laughs. I got a kick out of his stories, because he was a bit of a rebel and lived sort of a different life than I did. He would tell me some wild stories about his high school in Mississauga, while I would regale him with tales about hockey and life on the road.

We worked together one summer at an inn right near the cottage. Scott was a waiter because he was a year older. I was the toast boy in the morning and worked at the salad bar in the evening. I wore a bow tie, ugly brown pants and made $3.15 an hour. I remember Chef Lee was always ripping my head off over something. I was thirteen years old, and he would be flipping out because the toast wasn't cut totally straight or wasn't placed in the warmer the right way. The day usually started at six-thirty and we would go through about seventy loaves before breakfast was over. I had to butter it all with a paintbrush.

Someone would always order a special request during the crunch time. Now that was pressure. Whole wheat, no butter. I would think, "Why do they have to do this to me? Take the white bread with all the butter on it." Or they would send it back. "This bread's too soggy. It's been in the warmer too long." One time, someone complained that their buttered toast was soggy, and I tossed it back in the toaster. It started a little fire, which scared me a bit. The toast was burnt to a crisp, but it wasn't soggy anymore. It was a big relief sometimes just to get through the day.

The job had its fringe benefits, though. They had these massive bowls of Cool Whip and Jell-O and trays of banana cream pies in a huge fridge, and I used to lock myself in there and just fill my face. It's a wonder I didn't have to roll home.

My brother Brett used to deliver papers at the cottage to pick up some extra money. He would usually buy himself something nice at the end of the summer, like a bike or a Nintendo game. It used to drive me crazy to play Nintendo with him, because he would always beat me at it. After he won, he would look over and see me getting that look in my eyes, and he'd try to dash for the door before I could grab him. He rarely made it.

I'm trying to curb my competitive nature a bit. It's something that a lot of kids learn to do when they're three, but I'm finally learning. I always want to keep those competitive fires burning for hockey, but I don't mind so much anymore when I lose at sports like tennis. Still, when I go to a golf tournament and my team's in contention, I find myself saying, "Boys, sharpen up the shots here. Let's get it going."

Even as a little kid, competition always got me pumped up. My favorite TV show used to be *The Price Is Right*, because of the euphoric feeling of watching these people compete to win big prizes in the "Showcase Showdown." The contestants were bidding on trips or cars; they paid $100 to get a ticket to this show and they'd come away with $25,000 showcases. And they got to be on stage with big Bob Barker and all Bob's beautiful babes. It was a great show. I used to jump around all the time when someone won that showcase and tear down the stairs to tell my Mom all about it. She said my eyeballs were popping out. I still like watching *The Price Is Right*—it's my soap opera.

As far as sports go, I'm attracted to anything that puts me right on the edge. Water-skiing at the cottage really pumps me up. So much to gain; so little to lose. I just know when I'm going to make the big cut. Speed up the boat, really get it cookin'. The only time you're going to see me is when I pop up for air. I get right down there, right along the water, and all of a sudden my elbow gets caught in the water and I go flying down. Big deal. I'm right up again. If you start worrying about getting hurt, then you lose out on a lot of things in life.

Tobogganing at Doidge Park was a big thing in our family when I was growing up in London. It was lucky the park was so close to the hospital, because I was fearless. I would stand up on the toboggan and head straight for this wall of snow at the bottom of the hill, but I never tried to slow myself down. Smack! I would stumble around all woozy. Once I was bombing down the hill pointed directly at a park bench, and my Mom ran to stop the toboggan. My head collided hard with her knee. I went in for facial X-rays after that, but it did little to deter me.

The way I see it, even though the odds against you coming out on top might seem overwhelming in certain situations, you've got to take your chance or you'll never find out if it can be done. I've never been afraid to take risks—you've always got to tangle with that outside shot at winning.

7

Lamborghini Nights

> If you think you are beaten, you are.
> If you think you dare not, you don't.
> If you like to win, but think you can't,
> It's almost certain you won't.
> If you think you'll lose, you're lost.
> For out of the world we find
> Success begins with a fellow's will—
> It's all in the state of mind.
> If you think you are outclassed, you are
> You've got to think high to rise.
> You've got to be sure of yourself before
> You can win the prize.
> Life's battles don't always go

To the stronger or faster man.
But sooner or later, the man who wins
Is the man who thinks he CAN.

I carried a tattered copy of that poem to every game when I was a kid. My coach, John Futa, handed out the poem on little cards when I was eleven years old playing peewee hockey for the Toronto Marlboros. I didn't take it all that seriously at first, but it's something that has stayed with me through the years. And when I was fifteen and I started playing Junior B hockey, I began to realize, "This is good stuff, this is true, this is life." I could really see the value in it. I no longer have the card Mr. Futa gave me, but that's still my poem.

When I look at hockey, I think the mental aspect is about 60 percent of the game. If you think you can do it, you can. Just being physically fit and in A-1 condition to play is probably only 40 percent of the battle. Things start going sour when you begin to doubt yourself. So even when times are tough and my team is struggling, I'm confident. There's a fine line, because you want to be humble, not cocky or arrogant. But the best is just to be secure within yourself. The way that I'm secure and content is through knowing what I can do and believing in myself. I don't have any self-doubt on the ice.

As a player, I want to keep driving to reach levels I'd never before dreamed I could reach. I want to be the best I can be. I set my goals at a certain level and try to achieve those goals. Then I establish a higher goal, one that goes beyond the original objective. You just can't stop. When you get complacent, that's when you start losing your edge. I'm not happy about what happened last year, losing in the Ontario Hockey League finals against Sault Ste. Marie. I'll be back. You have to keep driving and striving.

I still have to work on every single facet of my game. I don't shoot the puck like Brett Hull, I don't skate like Paul Coffey, I don't think or set up plays like Wayne Gretzky, and I'm not as strong as Mark Messier. I may never reach the level of those players in any of those areas, but who's to stop me from trying, who's to say I can't? You can never be satisfied. I've got to learn more about everything—it's endless. No one knows everything about anything.

When I go to watch a hockey game, I focus on one player for a shift. I watch what he's doing, try to figure out what he's thinking. When Steve Yzerman curls, he turns on a dime. Messier, when he drives, his feet never stop moving. When Al Iafrate rushes, he doesn't care that he might get smoked, he just goes for it. You've got to like that. I look at what some guys do and I try to adapt it to my game. I try to integrate as much as possible. The more complete your skills are, the better a player you will be.

There was a sign in our dressing room in Oshawa: "The willingness to win is not as important as the willingness to prepare." That's so true, and it becomes more important as you move up through the levels in hockey. I talked to as many pros as I could this past year about what were the hardest things to adapt to coming in as a rookie. I don't think anyone can be prepared enough. You've always got to be receptive to other people's observations. Even if only one idea out of five is good, then you want to hear all five to get the one. If you don't go in knowing what to expect, you're going to get pushed around. And it doesn't matter what you've done in junior hockey, because you're starting from scratch in the pros. If you act like a know-it-all, the guys at the next level are going to look at you and say, "Who are you? You're just a rookie."

I've had to learn to pace myself a bit. I got in trouble at times last year for staying out too long on my shifts. You have to know when to go hard and when to slow down, otherwise you're going to burn yourself out early in the game and it will be impossible to rejuvenate. Sometimes, people say it looks like I'm coasting out there. But I'm not coasting; I'm thinking.

Mental preparation, being ready for every game, is the key. I know what I'm capable of doing, but being mentally prepared to do it, game in, game out, is sometimes where I falter. I have a hard time playing in the easy games. We beat Hamilton two years ago 9-1, but I didn't pick up a point and was a minus one in the game. I didn't play well and I just wasn't into it. But when North Bay came into our barn last year to battle for first place late in the season, our line was flying and I had four goals in a 7-4 win. That's the way it goes. Some games, everything just clicks and you can do no wrong. Other nights, it's "Who am I? Where am I? What time is it?" It's difficult to get motivated at times for games that might not be as important, but that's no excuse.

Confidence is something you build up over the years. I remember thinking, when we moved from London to Toronto, that I would be just a regular Joe on the ice. The hockey in London wasn't quite as competitive, and I was uneasy about how I'd measure up in my new surroundings.

I ended up on the Toronto Marlboros' atom team, and we won every single tournament we entered that year. The only thing we got edged out for was the league title, which we lost by a point. We had an awesome lineup, with several players who went on to play in the OHL—Grant Marshall, Nathan LaFayette, B.J. MacPherson, David Dorash. We were sort of a renegade team, and the other clubs really hated us. The parents of the opposing teams would curse us, but it never bothered us. We loved it; we ate it up. When they swore at us, we'd let them have it right back. Being ten-year-olds, we didn't always know what the words meant, but we used them because they were being used against us.

I was a defenseman back then, and I could pretty much do what I wanted with the puck, but that quickly changed when I began climbing up the ladder in the Metropolitan Toronto Hockey League. I often played in age groups with kids a year or two older, and there were times when it was difficult to keep up with the rest of the pack. Though I did all right and usually held my own, I was really nothing special.

Being the youngest on the team, I often had a hard time fitting in. A lot of people looked at me differently. I always hung around with the same guys year after year; there was a small group of us.

The peewee and bantam years were a struggle. I usually played up an age group, and for a couple of years, before my growth spurt kicked in, I was smaller than some players my own age. I would be skating as hard as I could, but I was moving like I had cement bags in my skates. Things reached a point, after I separated a shoulder, where I had to drop from minor bantam down to my own age group, pee wee. At times, I felt like a butterfly caught in a tornado going up against these larger and stronger players.

Ed Robicheau, my bantam coach when I was fourteen years old playing for the Toronto Young Nats, gave me a lot of confidence midway through the season. He starting putting me out on the ice for all the crucial situations, whether it was an important draw or we were shorthanded or on the power play. When the team was in a hole, he would look at me on the bench and say, "C'mon Eric, we need a big goal." For the previous three years of hockey, no one had ever said that to me. And it was all I needed to hear for inspiration, to feel deep down that I was the player to do it. Just hearing the coach say that one sentence, I would get my second wind right on the spot. He was the kind of coach who used to rant and rave and call you names that you had to ask your parents to translate for you later, but he could sure motivate you.

I had one other coach who loved to rant and rave—with just the opposite effect. If this coach had had his way, I would have been driven out of the sport when I was playing minor peewee for the Marlboros at the ripe old age of twelve. I didn't think anything could affect my love for the game then, but I really hated hockey that year.

We were just a bunch of young kids, but our coach ran the team like we were soldiers at boot camp. We had practices at 5:49 in the morning. I would ask him, "Why 5:49?" He'd say, "Eric, that extra eleven minutes makes or breaks the team." Well, he tried to break me all right. It was the first time I couldn't wait for a hockey season to come to an end.

OTHER VOICES:

Bonnie Lindros

It's supposed to be a kid's game—it's supposed to be fun. But we were all glad when Eric's minor peewee season with the Marlies was over. In our opinion, Ed Robicheau, who handled Eric's bantam team, had the perfect attitude for a minor hockey coach: his job was to look after the kids on the ice and the parents' would look after them the rest of the time. But one of Eric's minor peewee coaches had a different approach. He wanted every aspect of our lives to revolve around the team and the coaching staff. We were never given a master schedule of games and practices that season. Practices were held on any day and at any hour. It got to the point where the activities for the whole family revolved around Eric's hockey.

We seemed to be on a collision course with this coach from early on, and it wound up taking a real emotional toll on Eric. The season began on a bad note when the coach recruited five defensemen instead of the four he had promised when Eric signed up for the team. Having the extra defenseman meant that at least one kid was going to be spending a lot of time on the bench. It was hard for Eric because he was getting a lot more ice time on defense than his teammates. Understandably, they became frustrated, and he became the target for that frustration. When he came back to the bench after a shift, they would often mutter things like, "Make room for King Tut."

More than anything, though, we wanted to get Eric away from this coach because, in our opinion, he wasn't teaching values we could live with. At a tournament in Detroit that year, the Marlboros ended up playing a team from our hometown of Chatham. While he was with the Chatham Junior Maroons, Carl had played with the younger brothers of the opposing coach, Don Wakabayashi. Well, the Marlboros were so much stronger than Chatham that I guess our coach figured they could play without a goalie and still dominate the game. So they started the game without a goalie, left the net empty for almost the entire game and still whipped the Chatham team. But it was so degrading to the other team. Carl and I were just dying inside—I couldn't even bear to stay in the arena to watch. I said to Carl, "Put Eric in the Chatham uniform and we'll see how long our fearless leader plays without a netminder." Since we had only lived in Toronto one year and Carl and I had grown up in Chatham, I felt Eric's roots were deeper in Chatham than in Toronto. Carl walked up to Don Wakabayashi after the game and apologized because we both felt so terrible and embarrassed.

The situation with the Marlboros eventually became unbearable, and Eric left at the end of the year to join the Young Nats. We thought the season was behind us until we woke up on two separate occasions to find "Go Marlies Go" stickers plastered on our car and garage door.

During his first season with the Nats, Eric started receiving poison-pen letters. The first letter came in a big brown envelope with his name typewritten across the front. We thought it was a picture or a clipping from a tournament and saved it for him to open at the table after dinner. At his age, he was always excited about getting mail, but that was about to change. Inside the envelope was a poem typed in capital letters. As Eric read it, tears started streaming down his face.

> THEY USED TO SAY THAT HE WAS THE BEST,
> BUT NOW THEY ASK, "WAS HE EVEN DRESSED?"
> THEY DIDN'T NOTICE HIM DURING THE GAME,
> I GUESS ALL PEEWEE'S LOOK THE SAME!
> HE WANTS TO PLAY BANTAM, MIDGET AND "B",
> HE'S HAVING TROUBLE HANDLING LOWLY PEEWEE.
> HE SKATES AND MOVES LIKE HE'S 60 YEARS OLD,
> HE'S NEVER GOING TO MAKE IT—AND ABOUT TIME
>   HE'S TOLD!
> HAVE FUN WALLOWING IN MEDIOCRITY—PEEWEE!!

Poems started arriving regularly after that, all the verses filled with the same vindictive tone. Eric received five poems in all and was also sent a sympathy card at Christmas with the following inscription: "Special thoughts and heartfelt prayers are with you in your sorrow." At the bottom, in what appeared to be a kid's handwriting, was scrawled: "There is no shame in being cut from minor bantam. Perhaps next year you can play above peewee. P.S. Perhaps a heart transplant!"

After the poems started arriving, either Carl or I made sure we got home every day before Eric so that one of us could check the mail to prevent him from seeing another one. Finally, after threatening police action to those we felt were responsible, the letters stopped. It's sad the way some people lose all sense of proportion.

Carl Lindros

There's no question that things can get out of whack at times in minor hockey. Sometimes, when the kids get their equipment on, they look like gladiators on the ice, even at the atom and peewee levels. The parents and the fans sometimes go berserk, thinking that all of a sudden the kids *are* gladiators out there. Then when you see the players without their equipment on— even at the Ontario Hockey League level, when they're eighteen or nineteen—you realize they're just regular kids.

For some people, everything takes on so much importance. It seems to me some parents put an awful lot of emphasis on getting their kids on winning teams, which seems particularly odd if the kid is a defenseman or a goalie, because in that situation they're not really developing their skills to the maximum. It's best for a defenseman or goalie to be playing against stronger teams, where they're going to be challenged a lot. Naturally, Eric always wanted to play for a winning team, but we never put a high priority on that.

With Eric, we often had him play up an age level because we thought it was more important that he be pushed to develop his skills rather than that he be the best player on his team. If you're the best when you're twelve, it's kind of hard for you to keep working hard to be the best when you're thirteen. You have a tendency to start taking too many things for granted. Kids develop at different times. What's unfortunate about hockey is that kids aren't ever told, "Just because you're a hotshot now doesn't mean you'll be a hotshot later, so stick with the game, enjoy it, and work on all your skills." We never even looked at the standings when our kids were in minor hockey; the emphasis was on the pursuit. Being on a winning team wasn't as important as playing your best.

I know some coaches were upset when the kids played some extra hockey on a game day. But our view was that if it was just a regular league game, if you had an opportunity to play shinny for a couple of hours, you should play shinny as well as the game. You may not play as well in the game, but in the end you're going to be a better player. We were always thinking more long-term as opposed to how important each individual game was or looking at statistics.

We felt that finding a proper coach was really important, since their impact on the kids can be very broad. Besides being involved in such things as recruiting, organizing, skill instruction, discipline and motivation, the coach might be involved in talking to the kids about broader issues like drugs or sex.

Minor hockey is made up of a lot of volunteers from a cross-section of society. While most of the people get into it with some good in their hearts about what they're trying to accomplish, there are very few coaches who are perfect in all regards. When you think about it, who is perfect? The coach can start off with everything in balance, then, as the team gets closer to winning or is on the verge of losing in a big way, he can start to act emotionally as opposed to rationally. We're all human. The thing is not to assume that everybody or everything is perfect. As we discovered in that one difficult year, there can be a rotten apple in every barrel.

It was when I was fourteen years old playing in Junior B for St. Mike's that I started taking hockey a lot more seriously and began to see it as a possible future career. There were a lot of fans who used to come to our games, so the attitude sort of became, "We've got to put on a show here, let's get the line going." I would go home afterwards and talk with my family about the games. If I had a big game, where I played really well all over the ice, that was a "Lamborghini night." If it was just one of those games where nothing clicked, it was a "Lada night." It was just a contrast in cars and a contrast in the level of my play itself. The one sure way I could tell what kind of night I had was by the number of people waiting to talk to me after the game. If there was a crowd, it was a Lamborghini night. When it was just my parents standing there, I knew it was a Lada night.

I struggled at the start of Junior B, because I just couldn't put the puck in the net. It wasn't until halfway through the season that I caught fire and all the scouts and the media started coming out. I had a lot of help from Rick Wilson, the goalie coach at St. Mike's, assistant coach Tony Cella and also Harry McAloney. They spent a lot of extra time on the ice with me after practices, giving me the work I needed to sharpen my offensive skills.

One person who really helped me out at St. Mike's—and I will never forget him—was John McCauley, who passed away in June of 1989. He was the NHL's director of officiating, and his son, Wes, played defense for St. Mike's. Mr. McCauley taught me a few things about taking care of myself on the ice. I was getting my fair share of shots in Junior B, because I was fifteen years old playing against guys who were eighteen, nineteen, twenty years old. It got to the point where you had to learn how to handle yourself or you weren't going to be able to walk the next time you went to the rink. Mr. McCauley quickly identified the situation and he started teaching me some survival tactics. It wasn't so much dirty stuff but borderline things, like how you could discreetly grab the other player's sweater and twist him around without the referee noticing. He was always helping me out with pointers, and our families became good friends.

I only knew Mr. McCauley for one year, but it seemed to me his first priority was family and friends. I never saw him in a bad mood. He loved to come to our games at St. Mike's, and he would be beaming with pride as he watched his son Wes in action. One night at the arena, he said to my parents, "I've seen a lot of hockey games, but there is nothing more fun than watching your own kid play." He was always smiling, always cracking jokes. I remember when we had a surprise birthday party for my Mom when she turned forty. My Dad had ordered these huge trays of shrimp. Well, Mr. McCauley, my brother and I pilfered one and we hid ourselves at the back of the kitchen and the three of us wolfed down the whole tray.

It was pretty tough when he passed away. It was five days after the OHL draft, and it put things in perspective for me. Getting drafted to a place that wasn't going to work for me didn't seem so important after someone close to you passes away. Playing hockey's easy; it's life that's hard.

I had worn number 8 when I played at St. Mike's, and I later learned it was also John McCauley's number. When I got traded to Oshawa, I wanted to keep the number, but the captain, Iain Fraser, was wearing it. So I switched to number 88 and wore the same commemorative patch the NHL officials wore on their sweaters for Mr. McCauley that season. I still miss him. I went to a sports dinner this past year where they honored him. I just cried the whole time.

Everything seemed to come together for me as a player while I was at St. Mike's. Getting an opportunity to play two games with the Canadian Olympic team in December of that year gave me a real boost. I was fifteen at the time, the youngest ever to play for the Olympic team, and it was a little overwhelming at first. I was invited out by the team for two exhibition games in the Maritimes against a touring Soviet squad. The opposition wasn't exactly Krutov to Larionov back to Fetisov over to Makarov, but it was a good Soviet team, and I was really scared and nervous before the first game in Fredericton, New Brunswick. I was thinking, "These are men—they're going to be fast." I didn't know what to expect.

It was a whirlwind trip. I got home at 1:00 AM from a Junior B game against Peterborough the night before and was on a plane to New Brunswick with my Mom by 7:30 that morning. I had a cracked bone in my hand from a slash I had taken in the Peterborough game. My hand was really puffy and the Olympic team's trainer drained it before we went out to face the Soviets.

When we came out on the ice at the Aitken Centre, the fans went nuts and it was a bit intimidating. Here I am, coming from St. Michael's College School Arena, where we usually played in front of a couple of hundred fans, to a rink jammed to the rafters with nearly four thousand people. I needed to do something to get over my jitters and I found just the ticket—I scored on my first shift. It wasn't a great goal, but it really sent my confidence soaring. I got a quick chip pass as I was moving into the Soviet end and scored on a slapshot from the far side that caught the top shelf. For the first few seconds afterwards, I felt as if I were in another world.

When I went back to playing Junior B, my confidence level was sky-high and I started scoring a lot more. I also received an invitation to try out for the national junior team for the 1990 World Championships in Finland. The invitation alone pumped me up. I remember talking about it with Angelo Libertucci, our goalie at St. Mike's. He was really keen to get a shot at it, too, and we talked about how great it would be. But I never expected I would get the chance to do it.

I'd have some pretty heated battles during practice at St. Mike's with Angelo, whom we called "Tooch." I'd want to score so badly during the drills, and he was just as anxious to stop me. He would say, "You're not getting it by me, Eric." And I'd reply "Tooch, I'm getting it by you—it's going in." If he stopped me during a one-on-one drill, I would retrieve the puck and fire it into the net while he was getting ready to face the next player. Just to get under my skin, he would often let other guys put one past him and then say, "Eric, they scored. Why can't you score?" We had a lot of fun, but there was a serious competitive edge to it as well. If he stoned me in practice, it really bothered me the rest of the day. And if I was pumping them into the net, it really burned Tooch. It was a never-ending battle, and we loved it.

I'm intense when it's time to work hard in practice—I don't want anyone to beat me—but during some drills I'm laughing so hard that I almost fall over. I try to accomplish two things. I want to be happy and content, but do something productive at the same time. If you're not having fun, there's no sense being there. And having fun is something I love to do. I like to stir things up at practice. One of the little games we had at Oshawa involved trying to hit each other's skate blades with the puck when the other player wasn't looking. I used to do that through the whole practice. Our coach, Rick Cornacchia, would get fed up at times and finally say, "Will you guys just grow up!" But seconds later, I'd be banking the puck off somebody's skate blades again. Rick would just shake his head and laugh.

OTHER VOICES:

Rick Cornacchia
(head coach, Oshawa Generals)

Eric's ability to raise his level of play when there's something on the line is unbelievable. Eric becomes very focused. He hits harder, he skates harder—everything is turned up a notch. He can set the tone for the whole team by his play, which is a lot to ask of any individual. But because of the person that he is—he's respected by his teammates so much—if they see him busting his butt and finishing checks, the rest of the team falls in line and cranks it up another level. You can tell when Eric is really ready for a game. It's almost comparable to a racehorse who is chomping at the bit to get out of the start chute. You can really see it. His eyes are telling you, "Let me out, coach. I'm rarin' to go. Put me out there." When he gets into that mode, look out! He's going to blow the doors off someone.

When the Generals got the opportunity to make a trade for Eric, I asked Sault Ste. Marie for permission to meet with him. I wanted to get to know what type of person he was and to see how his presence would affect our hockey team if the trade worked out, since the chemistry of any team is very, very important. We got together for lunch and talked for about an hour and a half. One of the things I asked him was what he wanted to achieve if he came to the Oshawa Generals. He told me that his goals were to fit in and be accepted as one of the guys, and to contribute to winning a Memorial Cup. He didn't say that he wanted to score fifty goals; he didn't talk about personal accomplishments. Just by his presence and the way he carried himself, I believed what he said came from the heart. And after getting to know him, I know that's true. I told him at the time, "If we can make the trade and if I have any say in making the trade, then we're going to get you to play for the Oshawa Generals."

I just felt that he was going to make everybody on our team that much better, which turned out to be the case almost right from his opening practice. The whole team rose to the challenge when Eric arrived. His first time on the ice with us was on a Saturday afternoon before a game the following night against the Ottawa 67's, and it was the highest tempo practice I've ever run. The players were in a real state because expectations were so high after the trade had been completed. It was as if the team was saying, "Hey, we're going to show we can skate with this guy." The pace was so fast that I called the practice off after thirty-five minutes. I said, "That's it, let's save it for tomorrow." Eric raises the whole tempo of a practice, just like he can the tempo of a game.

It's not necessarily the amount of time you spend at practice that counts; it's what you put into the practice. You can skate forever, but it's no good unless you skate hard. I try to accomplish something at every practice. At the start, there's always a lot of team-oriented stuff, like working on systems and break-outs, but by the end of practice it becomes more individual. That's the time that you've got to take pride and do something productive. My attitude is, you're given the free time, don't blow it.

In Oshawa, our assistant coach, Larry Marson, would spend a lot of time after practice working with Robbie Pearson and me on things like one-timers—pivoting, winding and just firing the puck the second it touches your stick. We worked on that all season, but we spent the last three weeks before the playoffs last year really concentrating on those shots. Then, in the second game of the OHL final, I scored two goals from the far side of the rink on the exact same type of shot. It was an unbelievable feeling. I raised my hands to celebrate the goal, then thought, "We just practiced that." I went back to the bench and Larry had this huge grin on his face as if to say, "All right, Eric, you scored it, but you know who really scored it." It's a feeling you can't really explain. He knew it. I knew it. And we knew the source. It was him benefiting me and me helping myself and the team.

The same principles apply to any sport. When I went out for the baseball team at Henry Street High School in Whitby during my first year in Oshawa, I was brutal at the first practice. I hadn't played baseball in a while and I only hit three of ten pitches well during batting practice. My friend Jeff Hardy hit nine out of ten well, so I got him to pitch batting practice to me in the gym for an hour and a half later that afternoon. The next morning, I went eight-for-ten. I had to get better because I had embarrassed myself, and I knew the only way I could do it was through hard work and practice.

Creativity is one of the biggest things in hockey. If you're making the same move all the time, it's going to be easy for someone to get a read on what you're going to do. When you do something that is off the wall a little bit, something where people think, "Fat chance of this happening," that's when you usually get your best scoring opportunities. It's the element of surprise, because you're always keeping the opposition guessing. I'm not great at doing that, but I'm working on it.

If you're going wide the whole game, you're not going to be very effective in the second or third period, because they're going to know you're going wide. So, in the first period, you've got to curl and drop. In the second period, you've got to go wide. And in the third period, you curl, drop back and shoot. You've got to be different every time you come on the ice.

I do a lot of my thinking about strategy after the games. I can't sleep after a game, win or lose. I'm constantly replaying the game in my mind, settling down and thinking about the next one. I usually can't fall asleep until three in the morning. But after those games where I played really, really badly, I just go to bed.

One of the ways I prepare myself for a game is through visualization techniques. It's something that just came naturally about halfway through my Junior B season. When I go to bed the night before a game, I think about what I have to do in that game, how the other team plays against me, about the things they do well and also what they don't do well. I always think about positive things—taking someone out along the boards with a crunching check or scoring a couple of big goals. When you start thinking negatively, you get in trouble. Negative thoughts come in once in a while, but I do my best to block them out. There are a lot of times when I've visualized things and then they've happened in games, I have a lot of *déjà vu*. The more you practice, the more relaxed you become on the ice, and the easier the game flows.

I play little mind games with myself and I'm really superstitious. Everything's always left before right. When I get on a roll, if I had gum that game, I'm going to have gum for the next four hundred games—same amount of gum, same number of sticks. I get right into all the superstitions. My chain goes above my locker in the same spot, my coat and shirt hangers have to be pointed in certain directions. I always have coffee or Coke before the game, depending on which one's working for me at the time. It's the same with underwear. One of my friends, Lisa Best, painted some stuff on a pair of boxer shorts for me. If I wear those and have a good game, then I'll keep wearing them. (Of course, I'll get them washed every once in a while.) When you're struggling, you'll try anything. And when you get success, you keep that pattern.

The same pre-game ritual was followed pretty religiously in Oshawa. I'd put the fuel—lasagna, two buns and orange juice—in the furnace around two-thirty in the afternoon and then have a nap. One of the first things I did at the rink was work on my sticks, which always kept me busy for a while. After the team meeting, I would read the game notes in the same toilet all the time. It didn't matter whether I had to go to the washroom or not, I sat there until I was done reading. Then I would take the notes and toss them into Scott Hollis's stall. After some stretching and spending a bit of time in the trainer's room tending to the standard assortment of bumps and bruises, I'd have my coffee. Two cream, two sugar, in a little tiny coffee that tasted just like syrup. You know that the rituals and superstitions don't really do anything for you, but they keep you content inside, and that does a lot for you.

I like to prepare myself mentally for all possible eventualities in a game, including the chance that I might have to drop my gloves against one of the other team's tough guys. In my first year in the OHL, I was challenged to fight a lot. I held my own and did better than I was supposed to in a lot of respects, and the following year I wasn't challenged as much. There's a time and place for everything, and I knew I had to pick my spots. My job was to put the puck in the net and set up plays, not be in the penalty box. If it was a tight game, I wasn't going to risk it. But if we were leading 6-2 with two minutes to go and I was on the ice at the same time as the guy who's been running me all game, then that was the time and place. Rick Cornacchia would scream at me if I got into a fight in a close game, "Lindy, what are you doing fighting? You're letting everyone down!" As soon as he said that, the guys on the team would look at me and I felt like crawling under the bench.

On a lot of nights, I have to play a physical game or I'm not into it. I have to bang somebody; I'm not some little freelancer who can wheel and deal and not hit anyone. I don't perform at that tempo. I'm the type of player who has to antagonize a little bit. It's not a matter of playing dirty, just keeping guys alert, letting them know where you are. Watch Mark Messier when he loses a face-off. He lays a beating on the guy right there at the draw, and the guy doesn't want to come in to take the next draw. It's just the way he plays. Some people don't like it, but he wins the next face-off. Job's done.

The tone of a game can be changed with a devastating hit. If I try to crunch someone and I get knocked out, that's a big lift for the other team, so I've got to make sure the other guy goes down. And if I go down with him, that's fine, I've just got to make sure that I get up quicker than he does. That's what it's all about. Deck or be decked. There's a moment when you see someone charging up the ice, and he sees you. You make eye-contact with him and you both know that neither one of you is going to move out of the way. I'm thinking, "All right, you're in for a ride, you're going down. I might get hurt, but you're going to be hurt worse than I am." You've got to think you're invincible. If you're preparing to hit somebody, you can't be thinking that you're going to separate a shoulder. On impact, my body flexes and I try to draw power from my legs all the way up. It's a matter of timing; you have to lunge at just the right moment. When everything comes together and the other guy is sent reeling, you can just see the opposition bench sag.

In a game against Niagara Falls last year, I hit Andy Bezeau so hard that he went airborne and landed headfirst on the ice. Bezeau got right up, went to his bench and then walked down the hallway to the dressing room. He's a tough guy and he tried to show he was all right, but everyone knew that I hurt him. All the guys on their bench saw it, and it created enough space for me to have a really big night. I had a hat trick in that game, including my fiftieth goal of the season.

Apparently, I've always had a passion for the rough stuff. The first time I ever experienced bodychecking was at hockey school when I was about eleven. I don't remember much about it, but my Mom says I never touched the puck that whole scrimmage. I just ran all over the ice throwing checks, and when my turn was up, I would stand at the bench and scream, "Hit 'em, hit 'em." Bon says my face was purple and my neck veins were bulging. She was sitting there thinking, "Oh my God, this kid is whacko."

You find that you have to prove yourself at every level. When I was fourteen I was practicing with the St. Mike's Junior B team during my bantam year, and the other players would take shots at me all the time. I didn't always make the most of the situation.

I'd stick them or something like that and it would escalate, but I had to make a point. I almost got into a fight with Jeff Harding, who was a huge eighteen-year-old and a really tough kid. I figured, "What's he going to do? Bash out my teeth? My uncle Dan's a dentist. He can make me a new set." Some of the players might have thought I was a little crazy, but I got their respect.

Dan Cameron also helped me cope with the rough going in Junior B hockey. After my games at St. Mike's, I sometimes spent an hour or so talking with Dan, who was a former Junior B coach and then went on to coach Holland's national team for a few years. We went out on the ice together a few times, and one of the things he taught me was the nasties. The other players were taking liberties with me because I was a lot younger and I had to learn to handle myself. It's something you don't like talking about, but it's part of the game.

Hockey is a physical sport and fighting becomes a natural outlet for all the on-ice aggression. You're dealing with players in the heat of battle. What are you going to do, take them to *The People's Court* and sit them in front of Judge Wapner to settle their disputes? Judge Wapner doesn't have the time; there'd be just too many cases for him to handle. Other than the score, fighting can sometimes be the only way to settle matters.

8

For Pride and Country

Darkness in a public place can be hard to find, but darkness was just what I wanted.

Team Canada had one game left to play at the 1991 World Junior Championships, but I was sure that our gold medal dreams were cooked. We'd been through an emotionally exhausting roller-coaster ride against Czechoslovakia the day before. We'd been so close to winning, but we went off the rails in the closing minutes to lose 6-5. Our fate was no longer in our own hands. We needed Finland to beat or tie the Soviet Union in that night's game to give us a shot at the gold in our final game against the Soviets.

A lot of the guys on the team stayed at the hotel to watch the Soviet-Finland matchup on TV, but my teammate Brad May and I couldn't bear to watch and decided to go see a movie in downtown Saskatoon. I find something comforting about the darkness in a movie theater whenever I'm on the road. It's a chance to relax, a chance to escape the public scrutiny. You don't see the stares in the dark. I never like feeling as though I'm on display, but in this situation the desire for a little anonymity was greater than usual. I didn't even wear my Canadian team jacket out that night. No one did. I was proud of who I was and who I represented, but we were tired of the constant probing about what had gone wrong.

The expectations placed on us were immense. Canada had never won gold medals in back-to-back years at the World Junior Championships, but we were playing in our own country and it was built up as though a Canadian victory would be automatic. If we didn't win, then it would be viewed as if we'd let the whole country down. As our head coach Dick Todd put it, "It's win and be a hero or come second and be a bum."

As we sat in the theater, I was trying not to think about hockey, but my mind kept wandering. I couldn't help but wonder what was going on in the Finland-Soviet game. I knew that my parents hadn't given up hope. The whole family had made the trip to Saskatoon to cheer us on, and Carl had borrowed a Finnish national team hockey sweater to wear that day for a bit of good luck.

We had needed some outside help to win the world junior title the year before, too, and we got it when Sweden scored a goal with one second left to tie the Soviet Union on the last day. That lifted us into the gold medal position after we knocked off the Czechs 2-1 in a thriller. It seemed like too much to hope for two years in a row.

The movie did nothing to raise our spirits, but the ride back to the hotel provided an unexpected boost. Shortly after we slid into the back seat of the transport van, the score of the Soviet-Finland game crackled over the CB radio.

"Game's over. The Soviets 5 . . . Finland 5."

The Finns had come back to tie the Soviets with fifteen seconds left. Brad and I looked at each other in amazement and started pummeling each other on the back. Canada's gold medal dream was still alive!

The hotel was buzzing when we got back; the team was relieved to get another shot at accomplishing what we had set out to do back at that first training camp in August. The media, most of whom had buried us the day before, quickly resurfaced to get the lowdown on what we thought of our second chance.

The players and coaches got together for a team meeting in the hotel and the main message delivered was, "She ain't over till she's over." Any celebration was premature; the reality was that there remained a large obstacle ahead. The Soviets weren't just going to roll over and die. Finland might have opened the door for us, but we still had to step through it.

* * *

There's something indescribable about playing for your country. When you pull on that red-and-white sweater with the Maple Leaf emblazoned on it, you have a great feeling of responsibility. It's a sense that you're not just representing yourself, you're representing your country, your family and friends, your league and your team, your school, the variety store you go to, the place where you buy your gas. It may sound corny to some people, but it's true. I buy my gas at the same spot all the time and I always went to the same variety store in Oshawa before games. They all know me, I know them. In some way, we're all united. When people see you on television at a big event like the World Junior Championships, they feel part of it. They're thinking, "He comes to my restaurant to eat." "I sell him gas." There's a lot of nationalism involved, a sense of pride. Canadians can be

127

a pretty conservative bunch, but hockey gives us a chance to puff our chests out a bit.

Every time a Canadian team goes up against the Soviet Union, it's a battle for prestige in the world of hockey. It doesn't matter whether it takes place at the Olympics, Canada Cup, world juniors or the peewee level, the honor of Canada as a hockey nation is at stake. Nearly four million people across the country watched our final game against the Soviet Union—it was the biggest audience ever watching The Sports Network. There were guys sitting in bars in places like Flin Flon, Manitoba, and Glace Bay, Nova Scotia, watching the games, thinking, "I'm a Canadian. Those are our boys out there."

The fact that the 1991 world juniors were held in Saskatoon made that feeling of nationalism that much stronger. It just swept you up. I guess it was captured to a degree on televison, but it's really too bad that more people couldn't have experienced it. Everywhere you went wearing your national team jacket— whether it was to buy a pair of cowboy boots or grab a burger— people wanted to meet you and shake your hand. You couldn't get through the mall, because you meant so much to everyone.

I had a much better feeling about myself and my role with the team in Saskatoon than I'd had the year before at the 1990 world juniors in Finland. I'd been a little fish from a little pond going into a big ocean the first time around. I was sixteen years old, the youngest player in the tournament, and had been playing Tier II hockey with Compuware in Detroit. It was a really big step to suddenly be going up against the world's best. I was slotted in as a third-liner, a bump-and-grinder, and I was never all that comfortable with the assignment.

Building a winning team is like doing a puzzle—you have to find a way to put all the pieces together. When you do a puzzle, you start at the borders. The border pieces are critical. They're the glue that holds the whole thing together. Without solid border pieces in place, you're unsure how to put the rest of the pieces of the puzzle together. In my first year with the national junior team, I wasn't a blue-chip guy from any of the major Canadian junior hockey leagues, so I wasn't considered a border piece. I was just stuck into the middle of the puzzle somehow, and I never totally felt part of it.

Mike Ricci, who played for the Peterborough Petes at the time, was one of the team's border pieces in Finland, and he really helped me out. I roomed mostly with Mike, and he gave me a lot of confidence. He's a very calm and down-to-earth guy. When he signed his NHL contract after getting drafted in the first round by Philadelphia in June of 1990, he wasn't interested in getting a fancy car. He'd had the same car since he was six-teen, and that was good enough for Mike. As teammates go, you can't say enough about guys like him. They make it so much easier for players who have no experience and aren't on the same confidence scale.

Dave Chyzowski was a different matter entirely. Chyzowski, who played for Kamloops in the Western Hockey League, liked to pull pranks on the younger guys. He thought it was a real riot to do things like cut my skate laces and put Vaseline in Trevor Kidd's goalie mask. It seemed as if he was trying to make things as difficult as possible for me on the world junior team.

Chyzowski took another crack at getting me during the Memorial Cup later that year. He hit me from behind, knocking me headlong into the boards from about three feet out. That could have been my career right there, and I won't forget it. Another thing I won't forget was that the penalty call was only a two-minute minor!

Finland was a new experience for a kid who had never ventured much further than Buffalo. We stayed out in some cabins in the woods in a friendly little village called Berumaki. The accommoda-tions were great for the situation, but it was a bit like *Rocky IV*, where Rocky goes out into the winter wilderness to train for his big fight against the Russian heavyweight.

There wasn't much in the way of night life, which suited the coaches just fine. I'm not so sure that a bunch of teenagers away from home were as thrilled about it. They didn't have to worry about us chasing girls at night; the only thing you could chase out there was bears. The big thing at night was to have a bonfire. The menu, which consisted of a lot of reindeer stew, took a little getting used to. The guys were just salivating when we made our only trip to McDonald's. We had three different cashiers going at a furious clip. Whatever you couldn't eat there, you were taking back to the cabins.

On the ice, I gained more confidence as the tournament wore on. I was on a line with Steven Rice and Kent Manderville, and we were what you might call the designated hitters. "Ricer" is a great team player, a real mucker who's willing to do whatever it takes to win, and Manderville is exactly the same way. We're all big guys and we made sure our presence was felt—in a very physical way. Our job was to be an intimidating force out there, to put a scare into some of the stylish European players. We'd always go up against the big line from the other team, and our strategy was basically hit, hit, hit, hit. Ricer and I would come in behind the net and just demolish a guy. We'd almost be knocked out ourselves and we'd struggle to get back to the bench while they would still be lying on the ice. We managed to score our share of goals, though. I had four goals, which put me near the top of the team's list, and Ricer had a couple of goals. The coaches gave me more playing time as things progressed and I played better and better. I went from being a middle piece in the puzzle almost all the way to a border piece.

The whole tournament came down to our final game against the Czechoslovakians in a barn-like arena in the remote town of Turku. Not only did we have to win our game to claim the gold medal, but we needed Sweden to tie or defeat the Soviets in a game two hundred kilometres away in Helsinki. Not too many people liked our chances.

Well, we were doing our part in Turku with a 2-1 lead heading into the final minutes, courtesy of Dwayne Norris's second-period goal. Meanwhile, in Helsinki, the Swedes were endearing themselves to us forever with a stunning comeback. The Soviets were up by two goals with less than five minutes to play, but Sweden rallied to score two goals in four minutes, including the tying goal at 19:59 to make it 5-5.

The coaches got the news from Helsinki with about four minutes left in our game, but head coach Guy Charron decided it would be better if we didn't know. We soon found out, though. The Soviet-Sweden result came over the loudspeaker during a whistle with 2:46 left in the game, and the bench went wild.

I was standing on the bench beside Steven Rice and he was so intensely focused on the game we were playing that he didn't even realize what was going on.

"Ricer, you know if we win this game, we're going to be gold medal champions."

"Did you see that? Did you think that was offside?"

"Ricer, are you listening to me? Gold medal champions!"

"I still think it was offside."

The guys were all pumped when they heard the score from Helsinki. There was a lot of backslapping on the bench, but there was still a job left to do, and the guys were now more psyched than ever to do it. I don't think the puck left the Czechoslovakian end much after that. We were now going for the GOLD, and we got it.

We went crazy when the buzzer sounded to end the game. It was such an incredible turn of events. We stood at the blue line and belted out "O Canada" from the bottom of our lungs—forgive us if we were more than a little off-key.

It was a great win, but I couldn't escape the feeling that I could have contributed more to the team. I wasn't disappointed. I had really done more than my job, and it's when people do more than their jobs that you're successful. Everyone did more than their jobs on that team. But if I don't feel that I've played a key role in the team's success, then I don't feel as much a part of it.

*   *   *

After the experience in Finland, I was determined to be the first border piece laid down when they started putting together the puzzle for the national junior team that would play in Saskatoon. I knew that Dick Todd, who was an assistant coach at the championships in Finland, would be leading the team in Saskatoon, so I used every available opportunity to make the proper impression on him. My first big chance came in the Ontario Hockey League playoffs that year when we squared off against Dick's team, the Peterborough Petes. We blew Peterborough away in four straight games. The following season, we rolled into Peterborough shortly before we left for the world juniors and we bombed the Petes 9-2. I was trying to get my Oshawa linemate Robbie Pearson on the team, too. Our line had a big night: I had three goals and two assists; Robbie scored another two and added three assists; and Matt Hoffman played a solid game, too. It was like sending a message: "Dick, remember this." So when we got to Saskatoon, one of the first things Dick told me was, "All right, you're our gunner." That was just what I wanted to hear. I was ready to crack open the barrel of my shotgun, put in my round and go for it. We were all ready to take aim, and we had a gold medal lined up in our sights.

We had a good nucleus returning from the team that won in Finland. Mike Craig, a teammate from our Memorial Cup winning team in Oshawa, now on loan from the Minnesota North Stars, was a border piece. Goaltender Trevor Kidd was another border piece, as were my old linemates from Finland, Steven Rice and Kent Manderville. There was a good feeling at our first training camp. We were thick as thieves. Dick Todd was showing a lot of faith in us, and we didn't want to let him down.

I really enjoyed playing for Dick, because he's so competitive, even off the ice. We played volleyball between games in Saskatoon and, to avoid injuries, the rule was that you had to play sitting on your butt. You weren't allowed to stand. Meanwhile, Dick was cheating left and right, lifting his butt off the gym floor. He would be yelling at guys if they weren't digging for the balls hard enough. Dick wanted to win. Dick's team won.

Dick and I had some pretty good running battles in the OHL. We're both so competitive that we'd say anything to rattle one another, do anything to win. He would be shouting, "You're nothing! You're nothing!" and I would be getting in some personal digs at him. I found out he used to work in a supermarket stocking shelves, so I'd yell back, "Hey Dick, go shelve some stock, buddy! What are you doing here, Dick?" It would go back and forth all game. But then you go to work together on the national junior team and you're one, a tight little unit.

Dick's old-fashioned in some respects, but it's great to play for him. He understands you. He treats you like a person. It's like playing for your uncle.

Dick was a pretty protective uncle during the lead-up to the world juniors, and he had to be. There was a huge amount of media attention, and Dick and his assistant coaches, Alain Vigneault and Perry Pearn, did their best to keep us under wraps. We held our final training sessions in Kindersley, a small farming community southeast of Saskatoon. We were there to keep ourselves focused on the job at hand, and I think we were more than focused. We went to bed at 10:30 PM on New Year's Eve (my brother Brett had fun cutting me up about that). All the phone calls we received were monitored so that only family and close friends could get through, and only at certain times, and they also made sure we couldn't be bothered when we were trying to sleep.

The people in Kindersley were just super; they would do anything for you. We went to the mall and we asked if we could borrow a stereo system for our dressing room and they happily obliged. We often had the tunes blaring during the intermissions of our games.

The same community involvement was there in Saskatoon. There was a corps of volunteers who did everything possible to make our parents and brothers and sisters feel part of the event. It really helped to rally everyone behind the team. Everybody recognized that it was on the line, that everybody wanted to be at their best, that there was a lot of pressure and there was a lot we would have to overcome.

There was a real sense of camaraderie and patriotism among the families. The efforts of Brad May's family were pretty special, though. Brad didn't see a lot of ice time in the tournament, but he was really the heart and soul of the team. He was told the night before the final game that he probably wasn't going to play. He was devastated, and so were his parents, but they were the ones who made the arrangements to get the huge Canadian flag that was splashed all over television screens across the nation. My brother Brett and Brad May's brother Darryl and stepfather Doug got up at the crack of dawn to go to a car dealership to borrow that flag for the final game against the Soviets, and then they went to a fire hall to get a megaphone.

All the brothers and sisters really got into the spirit for the game. Many wore stetson hats and had their faces painted in the red and white of the Canadian flag. Brett, Robin and Darryl dressed up in white painter suits covered with the Maple Leaf and with the names of the players scrawled on their pant legs.

Brad May and I had a good laugh when we caught a glimpse of them in the upper deck before the national anthem.

The road to the gold medal showdown with the Soviets was certainly a rocky one. It took us a while to gel as a unit; we just weren't playing as a team at the start. We nearly got knocked off by the United States in our second game but bounced back to escape with a 4-4 tie. Sweden also had us down after two periods before we finally put it into gear to beat them 7-4.

We really got fired up before the third period in the game against Sweden. All the boys who were leaders got excited. We were all mad at each other, mad at ourselves, because we were a much better team than we were showing. We knocked the stick rack over, broke a few sticks. We got the stare going. I have a lot of stares that I use to psych myself up and to get the team psyched. It's a look that shows, as soon as you walk in the room, that it's all business. Guys joke around and all that, but if you portray that image and mean it, then it rubs off on them later on. It's a look that says, "If I'm ready, you better be ready because I'm not wasting my time if you're not there." You're only as good as the other people on the ice, so you've got to make sure they're ready, too. After we tossed a few things around in the dressing room and had our little discussion, Dick Todd came in and didn't have to say much. We had delivered the message to each other loud and clear, and we went out and won the game in the third period.

I was playing on a line in the tournament with my former Oshawa Generals teammate Mike Craig and Pierre Sevigny, a forward from the Quebec Major Junior Hockey League. We were the snipers. I really got a charge out of Sevigny, whom we called "Pete." He was a real instigator on the ice. He'd go into the corner, bump and grind, and all of a sudden he would be lying on the ice grabbing his cheeks as if someone had stuck him in the face. He had a full face-mask on so there was no way that someone could get their stick under his chin-guard, but Pete drew penalties that way. He was a great guy to play with, although I must admit our communication wasn't the greatest. We would say, "Pete, Pete, we're going to play two guys in and one guy back." He'd say "Okay, okay." Craiger and I would go in after the puck and, whoosh, Pete would be right in there with us. We'd just go scrambling back.

The media scrutiny throughout the tournament was really intense. At times, I thought they were trying to pull our team apart when we weren't doing well. You had to keep your cool. A lot of reporters were looking for any little bit of controversy. The press just ripped our goalie Trevor Kidd apart after we lost to Czechoslovakia and it looked like our gold medal hopes were gone, and the defense really came under fire too. They took their fair share of cracks at me, but I was used to it. I preferred that they use me as their target. A lot of guys were under some stress.

I really felt sorry for Kidd, whom I had become good friends with during the world juniors the year before. "Kidder" is an innocent kind of guy. He's like most goalies; he's a different dude. He's in his own world, and that's something I could relate to. We got along great, because I think we're in sort of the same world. I couldn't just sit there and let Trevor take a beating like he did. They were trying to make him the scapegoat. One TV reporter after the Czech game asked Trevor, "What sort of a burden does this put on you personally?" I talked back to the reporters and I said, "I can't believe you guys are doing that to Trevor Kidd. I don't think that's fair, I think that's inappropriate." I said it into the cameras and I said it to everyone, but not one of the reporters used it because I was cutting them up professionally. Dick Todd also took a lot of heat. We both tried to act like sewer systems for all the garbage that was getting heaped on us.

When you're a goalie, so much of your success or failure has to do with confidence. When you're hot, you're hot. And when you're not, you've got to get right back up again. When things aren't going so great, why cut someone apart whose position relies on confidence? If you want the country to win so badly, why not show a little compassion and support? We knew that the only chance we had of winning the tournament was to back each other all the way, and that's just what we were determined to do.

Dave Harlock
(teammate, world junior team)

I think the pressure was to the greatest extent on Eric's shoulders. He was the kid who was supposed to be the leader on the team. He had played on the world junior team the year before, and everyone expected him to guide Canada to its second World Junior Championship. The fact that it was in Canada only heightened things that much more. The media also really hyped the tournament as a head-to-head confrontation between Eric and Pavel Bure of the Soviet Union, since both were considered the top junior players in the world.

I had played Junior B hockey with Eric in Toronto at St. Mike's when he was fifteen years old. I really marvelled at the fact that he handled the early exposure he got there so well, especially since he was playing against and with players as much as six years older. Yet when I look back at the amount of exposure he got at the world junior tournament—which dwarfed anything he had at St. Mike's—he still handled himself in the same mature way. It's hard to believe he was seventeen at the time.

137

He really epitomizes everything you would want in a leader. At times, he can go out and be a pure leader on the ice. He can change the flow of a game in his team's favor just by making a good hit, taking a hit, making a good pass or scoring a big goal. In the same sense, he's a leader off the ice. He's good in the dressing room, he's good at motivating kids on the team. His presence really pulls people up; it makes them play to their potential, because you realize you are playing with Eric Lindros. In all cases, he's going to do the best he can. If everybody else goes out and does that, you're obviously going to be successful. That's the whole aura behind him.

During the world juniors, he would come up to me before a lot of games and say, "If I'm not in this game, yell at me or do something to annoy me, to get me motivated." He always wanted to be in a situation where he was playing at his best. And if he wasn't playing at his best and was struggling, he always wanted someone to do something that would give him a spark to get him going. He knew he was an integral part of the team and there were a lot of expectations of him. He didn't want to let anybody down. He didn't want to let the team down, he didn't want to let himself down. There weren't many times—if any—when I had to say something to him, but it made me want to do better, too. If Eric Lindros is telling me to help make sure he's ready, then obviously he expects that of everybody.

When we lost to the Czechs and it looked like it was all over, that was really hard to deal with, since all of Canada expected us to win the gold. I think it was even harder on certain individuals, Eric among them, because he was set up to be the fall guy if we lost. We knew after the Czech game that we had no say whether or not we won the gold medal. We had to rely on somebody else to do us a favor—and, fortunately, Finland did just that. Suddenly, we had a second chance to do what we wanted to do. I think everyone on the team felt relieved, but I think, in the same breath, everyone knew the pressure was back on our shoulders.

There was a lot of uncertainty in the dressing room before the Soviet game. Everyone was trying to convince themselves that the pressure was on the Soviets. Guys were saying the Soviet Union could have won the gold medal last night and they didn't, so they're the ones who should be feeling all the heat. But that outlook changed the second we stepped on the ice before more than eleven thousand truly pumped-up fans at SaskPlace. Everybody was dressed up in red-and-white and waving Canadian flags. No one on the team really said anything, but we pretty much realized all of Canada was behind us and everyone still expected us to beat the Soviet Union and win the gold medal.

Both teams were tentative at the start of the game, because we were the ones who had been given the second chance and they were the ones who had blown their chance. I think both teams were concerned with what the other team was going to do rather than just going out and doing what they were supposed to do.

Pierre Sevigny gave our team a wake-up call five minutes into the game when he scored off a rebound. I had made a rush from our end and tried to stuff the puck past the Soviet goalie from the short side. He made the stop, but Pete was right on the spot to tap it in. I think it was Sevigny's goal that kicked in confidence. That goal put us on Cloud Nine. From Cloud Nine, we were ready to go through the solar system. But there was some tough going ahead before we could take off into orbit.

Steven Rice scored to give us a 2-0 lead after the first period, but the Soviets fought back to tie the game early in the third. Just as it was in Finland a year before, one of the boys from the Rock came through for us in the clutch. John Slaney, a defenseman from St. John's, Newfoundland, took a shot from the blue line. It bounced off something and went into the Soviet net. "Yes! Whoa!" The crowd just exploded. The goal came just when we were starting to tire and they were taking it to us. We were now just over five minutes away from victory, but the job ahead was not an easy one—keeping the hard-charging Soviets off the scoreboard. I looked over my shoulder at Dick Todd to let him know our line was more than eager for the task.

Dick Todd
(head coach, world junior team)

Having been in the coaching business for eighteen years, I have a keen sense of when a player on the bench starts to turn his head to let you know that he really wants to be out there. He doesn't say anything, but it's clear he's looking for the opportunity to be used in that pressure situation. I think Eric's one of those few people who want to be out there, be it success or failure, to make it happen. You have to have a feel for that. There are certain athletes who are ready to do that for a team.

It's like Reggie Jackson going to the plate with the score tied 2-2 in the bottom of the ninth. He thinks, "This is my chance to shine." As coaches or managers, you put your best pitcher on the mound, your best hitter up to bat. What's going to happen? Is the hitter going to make contact and knock it out of the park? Or s the pitcher going to strike him out? I think Eric senses the moment when it's necessary to produce. Then he comes up with that big play, because he is what he is.

When I was putting the team together, he had a very strong curiosity from the beginning as to whether he was going to be given that role. He wanted to know, "Am I going to be on the ice at critical moments?" You know you're going to use him in that situation because he's a player who gives you the feeling that you can win anything. He was focused and wanted to win right from the first August training camp. He wanted to make a contribution to a gold-medal-winning team that maybe he felt he hadn't made the year before. And he didn't want to fail. In the summer practices, a lot of guys go out on the ice and just want to have fun, and think that they're automatic choices. He wasn't one of those guys.

When we got to Saskatoon, we were counting on him heavily. Instead of being just a player, he was going to be *the* player. As a result, there was a lot of weight on his shoulders from the public and the media. Most people don't watch and wait for success; they watch and wait for failure. When it comes to Eric, people are so quick to say, "Oh, this guy's not as good as everyone says he is." I still go out on the street today and people will say to me, "Well, he's not that good. I watched him. He looks kind of lazy out there." I think the nature of our mentality is to look for someone to fail to live up to the expectations that the press has created.

My concern in Saskatoon was that I didn't want to burn him out. It was important that he have the strength and power necessary for the final game. As a coach, you have to hold a player back at times, you have to make sure he has something in reserve down the stretch. It's the same as a jockey rating a racehorse for a mile-and-a-half race. The one that gets out of the gate first and jumps into the lead is not always the one that finishes first. There was no question that Eric was our biggest and strongest and most adaptable player, best able to handle the situations that we were involved in. That's the reason I gave him the nod to hop over the bench when the game was on the line against the Soviets. He probably played four of the last five minutes and took all the face-offs. In that situation, you want your best out there.

Dick Todd just sent our line on the ice to stay. If the Soviets were going to score, they would have to pay a helluva physical price, because we were prepared to do anything to stop them. There was no way I was going to get tired. I was far too psyched. I was on my ninth wind. Dick would check once in a while to make sure we could all keep going.

"You all right?"

"Yeah, I'm all right!"

"Craiger, you all right?"

"Damn right, dude!"

Craiger's one of those ride-the-wave dudes.

Alain Vigneault, our assistant coach, would check on Pierre Sevigny.

"*Es-tu fatigué?*"

"*Non, non, non!*"

I thrive on playing in the crucial moments of a game. I like to be in the thick of things. Even when I'm not at 100 percent, I just feel I can do more than the next person in that situation. It's that desire, a matter of wanting it so badly. You've got to think no one wants it more than you. I've always felt that way.

When I was a ten-year-old kid playing atom hockey with the Toronto Marlboros, I would tug on the sleeve of my coach's jacket during the big games and say, "C'mon, let me out there."

It's the same thing I did with Dick Todd, or my Oshawa coach, Rick Cornacchia, except that I can't tug on their jackets. I give them a look that lets them know I want to be out there. I'm not a spectator, I'm not a bench-warmer, I'm a player. I like the heat. I like stress. I love it when the stands go nuts. Everyone's yelling and screaming. It's a combination of things. It's just anxiety, fear, confusion, and it's fun. The fun part is knowing that you're going to come out on top. I always think that way: what's the point of going into a stressful situation with second thoughts? You've always got to go in positive.

Playing against the Soviets in the dying minutes of the game was serious heat—it was a downright scorcher. I took five draws in our own end. I won the first three draws, then I lost one. I was so upset with myself for losing the draw that I didn't take out their centerman. He went for the net. They tried to get a shot on net. There was a mad scramble. Just lay lumber on anything and anyone. Here we go!

I kept looking at the clock. You could see all the players peeking up at the scorebard. The last few minutes seemed like an eternity. It was heat, but it was fun. I'm thinking, "This is your association for the rest of your life. You are on Canada's gold-medal winning team for 1991. I was a member of the team that won the year before. You're something in Canadian history." That's what it's all about. We've got to win.

Finally, the last few seconds were ticking away. I had a countdown of my own in my head, but it had nothing to do with numbers. H-I-S-T-O-R-Y.

As soon as the game ended, Brad May and I grabbed each other in a bear hug like we were never going to let go and toppled to the ice. We were screaming "We're the best! We're the best!" Brad was the piece of the puzzle that made the team work. He would get out there twice or three times a game and hit anything that had a heartbeat. He was a team player all the way.

We went back to congratulate Trevor Kidd. He had played such a great game. The press had put his neck out so far and were trying to chop his head off, but he showed what he was made of in that final game. Kidder just said "Thanks." That one-syllable word meant so much.

Dick Todd came up as I was sitting there on the ice.

"Dick, we did it again!"

"We're great, aren't we!"

It was a wonderful feeling, but the most overwhelming emotion was probably relief. The pressure that had been placed on us was really incredible. It would have been such a disappointment to everyone if we had lost. The reason the gold medal was ours was that we were united as a team.

I remember being at the news conference afterwards with Dick Todd, Pavel Bure and the Soviet coach. Pavel was crying. The press tried to make the tournament into a big competition between me and Pavel. I wasn't into that; it was something I didn't need. It was our team against their team. I'm not a single gold-medal player. It's not like tennis—this is a team competition. Pavel scored a pile of goals, and he's a very good player, but he and his coach fought the whole time. We hung together as a team and supported each other. That's the best part about team sport. Even when things got tough, we didn't start pointing fingers. It was controlled emotion. We didn't get too feisty, but people knew: you mess with one, you mess with us all. We won because we stuck together.

9

Bird on a Wire

I was out at a batting cage in Oshawa two summers ago, shortly after we won the Memorial Cup, trying to work on my swing and relax a bit after a long and exhausting season. Like a lot of people in the city, I was wearing a Memorial Cup baseball cap, the brim pulled down low to keep the sun out of my eyes. I was just getting into my rhythm when one of the kids waiting his turn decided to strike up a conversation. He was a hockey fan and, as I would soon discover, quite a critic. But he didn't recognize me.

"The Memorial Cup was a big disappointment, eh?"

I was pretty taken aback.

"What do you mean?" I asked him. "Oshawa hasn't won in forty-six years, and they won the Memorial Cup."

"But Eric Lindros didn't even get a goal."

"Yeah, but he played really well," I countered.

"Nah, he only got assists."

"Yeah, but he got NINE assists. He played REALLY well."

"Oh, sure, and where were you sittin'?" he asked, his voice full of sarcasm.

"On the players' bench."

"Oh yeah, sure, and I bet you started the game, too."

"As a matter of fact, I did."

The guy looked at me quizzically for a second.

"Who are you?"

I lifted my cap up, and he just about fainted. He hightailed it out of there pretty quick; you couldn't see him for dust.

He wasn't the only one to offer his unsolicited opinion on my performance at the Memorial Cup. I had 18 goals and 36 points in 17 playoff games that year, picked up nine assists in four games in the Memorial Cup and contributed to a championship team—yet the first thing a lot of people said to me was, "You didn't score any goals in the Memorial Cup." A lot of them didn't mean anything by it, but some did. One thing I've certainly learned is that you can't please everyone.

I really get the feeling that there are a lot of people out there who want to see me fail. A lot of people want to see me succeed—don't get me wrong—but I'm not exactly loved by everyone on this planet. There are a lot of expectations, but I don't care. All you can ask of yourself is to try to do your best, the most that you can do. And if you can come close to doing your best, then that's pretty good. The satisfaction always has to come from within.

To be honest, I never really expected to get this far in hockey. I actually thought I'd go through school and be a marketing analyst or something like that. I wanted to be a policeman when I was younger. I kept changing what I wanted to be, but I remember mostly thinking about being a cop. Ever since I was a kid, I've liked speed, and cops get to drive fast. I also thought about being a lawyer, but then I realized all the reading that would require, and I wasn't up for it. Books are not my passion—hockey is.

There were some nights in junior hockey, though, when I really wondered whether I wouldn't rather have been out somewhere pounding a beat. I mean, junior hockey can be abusive. On some nights in certain arenas, I would take harrassment from fans in the stands throughout the whole game. Grown men and women would yell and swear at me, throw things at me and spit on me—and some could do it all at the same time.

Playing in North Bay was always an interesting experience. The first time I played there, someone ran an advertisement in the newspaper a few days before the game encouraging the fans to make degrading signs about me and boo every time I stepped on the ice. It turned out to be a pretty rough game—one player gave me a two-hander across the head, and my teammate Mike Craig had his leg broken in an incident that resulted in a seventeen-game suspension for the other player. I remember telling my family later that week at dinner about how the fans had acted. I was sixteen and still pretty upset by the experience. Brett just looked at me and said, "And you didn't moon them, Eric?" I started to laugh and immediately felt better.

When I got a penalty in North Bay, the whole place would go nuts and some sections would give me a standing ovation. I'd give a little bow, go into the penalty box, say hi to everyone. They'd spit on me. I'd duck. It's the just the way it was. I came out of the rink in North Bay once and I was signing some autographs for a group of kids when a couple of forty-year-old ladies walked by to deliver a message to me. "You suck s——t." I said, "Thank you very much, ma'am," and I just continued signing. In Cornwall, when we beat the local team, the fans took the armrests off the chairs and threw them at our bench. I guess there's no questioning the loyalty of the fans to their teams, and I'm sure the crowds in Oshawa could be equally abusive to the opposition, but some people really get carried away.

One night, in Kingston, the crowd was throwing stuff all over me as I headed to the dressing room, because we had won the game and there had been a couple of fights. One kid threw a full, jumbo cup of Coke right at me. I saw it coming and caught it, with barely a drop spilled. I motioned the kid over to me: "Come here, I think this belongs to you." And I handed it right back. His mother sent him down to the dressing room later to apologize.

It's usually the adults who cause all the trouble, though. Grown men and women will yell everything in the book at you, and the kids follow suit. The kids don't even understand what they're saying in most cases. If these adults ever sat down and really thought about what they were saying and how they were acting, they might think twice about it. Maybe they don't realize these are just kids they're spitting on and abusing. Most of the kids playing junior hockey are teenagers; they're just going out there and trying to have some fun at a game they work hard at. Sometimes I get the impression that it's the highlight of someone's day to go out and verbally abuse a bunch of kids trying to do a job on the ice. It's as if it makes them feel a lot bigger. It's like Yuk Yuk's Comedy Cabaret on Friday night in Sudbury. "Let's go to Yuk Yuk's at the Sudbury Arena, dump all over Eric Lindros and laugh." Sometimes, you just feel like saying, "Get a life, leave me alone. Leave the rest of the team alone. Just let us play."

This past summer, there were a number of incidents where athletes started going after fans who were heckling them. If I went into the stands every time I was irritated, I would never make it onto the ice. My skates would always be getting sharpened. You just can't let it affect you, because it's always going to be there. But somehow, there has to be some kind of line drawn for what's considered acceptable behavior. And the cops have got to take people out when they cross that line.

I guess the question is, where do you draw the line? There's a gray area there. The fans pay for their tickets; they've got the right to free speech. But I think throwing stuff is dangerous. A player or official can step on a penny and it could end his career. Name-calling is going to be there, but sometimes people get really personal and take it too far.

Then there are the signs that fans hang in the arenas. Some people can get carried away, both pro and con. In Oshawa, some girls hung up a banner: "On the Eighth Day God Created Eric Lindros." And when I played in Cornwall, they countered with a sign declaring: "If Eric Lindros is God, I want to go to hell."

Bonnie Lindros

People dish out meanness in different ways, but I'm sure they were very critical of Wayne Gretzky and Mario Lemieux and every other good player. That goes with the territory, and you have to learn to cope with it. I think the press can be very mean, too. Vicious at times. The people who criticize me won't say anything to my face. They have to do it through Eric or their columns. That, to me, is so spineless. If they've got something to say to me, I wish they would just go ahead. We'll discuss it. If I'm wrong, I'll admit it. It shocks me sometimes when I read what's written about us in the newspapers, because I can't imagine people being that mean or thinking that meanly. I'm getting used to all the potshots, but I don't like it. The abuse is always directed at me. Why can't they send a little more Carl's way? He's got big shoulders. He's six-foot-five and 240 pounds—maybe that's why they leave him alone.

Eric wants the fanfare and the fun, so he has to pay the price. It's a two-sided thing. Hopefully, he's got his values firmly planted. It bothers me sometimes that he has extra money so he can go to restaurants for meals rather than make something for himself at home. I don't want him to get so fancy that he can't scramble an egg in the frying pan if he's hungry—he used to scramble *six* eggs in the frying pan. He has his chores at home that he's responsible for. I recognize that he has a lot of stress in his life at times, but that doesn't mean he can't sweep the floor or do the dishes. I don't want the glitz to affect him.

I think Eric will handle everything just fine. He'll get tougher and he'll also recognize people's weaknesses because he recognizes his own, and he won't be afraid to say what he thinks. There have been some tough things for him to deal with as a teenager, but I think you gain a strength from adversity. I just wish that Eric hadn't had to do so much living already in his short life.

It's funny, but there's no big thrill to all the attention. It can get uncomfortable when I'm out with my friends, because I don't like feeling as if I'm on display. When I go to a restaurant, I never sit against the wall; I always eat with my back towards everyone else, so that I don't notice the stares.

When I went out with the boys in Oshawa after the game, everyone in the restaurant knew you were there, they knew how long you were there, they knew exactly what you ordered. I often feel as if I have to watch everything I do, everything I say and be careful with every step. My friends have started calling me

"Grampa." I've had that type of scrutiny pretty much since the junior draft and all the controversy with Sault Ste. Marie. I always try to be in control of the situation when I go out and to anticipate trouble brewing the way I do on the ice. I tend to go to the same places every time, because you get to know everyone, they treat you really well, and you never have any problems.

I tried to stay away from going out on week nights with the boys, because if you're out partying all the time, then people obviously get the wrong perception of you. And I've always made sure to steer clear of people who use drugs. No one has ever come up and offered me drugs, because they know I'm not interested. I smoked cigarettes twice at the cottage with my friend Scott Bailey, but I didn't enjoy it and have never tried it since. I've seen people taking drugs, but I'm very naive about the situation. As far as I'm concerned, there are better ways to get high. I'd rather get a high from winning.

There aren't too many nights I'm out that I don't run into some autograph-hunters. The memorabilia boom has been overwhelming. It seems that everyone wants something signed, and hockey cards aren't just for kids anymore. It's got so out of hand that a twenty-one-year veteran police officer was charged with discreditable conduct for allegedly selling cards of me that were supposed to be given out free to kids. When I was nine years old, my friend Grant Marshall and I spent an afternoon at his kitchen table practicing our autographs like we were going to be big-league hockey players, but I never imagined the training would come in so handy.

Our coach in Oshawa, Rick Cornacchia, always knew the bus was going to be slow leaving when the Generals were on the road, because I would be busy satisfying autograph requests. I wanted to sign everyone's pictures or cards or pieces of paper, so that no one was left out. I try to please them all. One time, in Oshawa, we had an autograph session and they didn't have anything organized. People stampeded forward and I kept getting pushed further and further back until I ended up sitting on top of a Coke machine because I was worried about getting crushed.

It's not always that dangerous, but it can get pretty hectic. I get approached for autographs at restaurants, often when I'm in the middle of a meal. I always sign, but I usually ask if they'll wait until I'm finished eating. At movie theaters, there are times when pieces of paper start flying back—people pass them row by row. I sign them and I pass them back. It's fun, but there's also a limit to what you can take. I'm human, too, and I get cranky at times. You can't always be as jovial as you'd like. I do my best, but people are always going to judge you and there's nothing you can do about it.

I get a fair bit of fan mail and I try to keep on top of it. It might take me a while to respond, because I do my own—with a big assist from my brother and sister. (I apologize if I've ever messed someone's up.) I really get a charge out of some of the stuff. I get a lot of pictures of myself drawn by little kids, some neat poems, and a girl from Ottawa sent me a cassette with a song she wrote about me on it.

It can get a little bizarre, as well. A guy from Sudbury once came up to me and popped a huge hunting knife out of a bag— he'd made it himself—and handed it to me as a present. I've had women send me some pretty wild nude pictures of themselves; I've had about eight of those. And I've had proposals to go to certain cities "for a good time." Whether it's these women sending the letters or someone else pulling a prank, I don't know, and I'm not about to find out, either.

I don't have a steady girlfriend right now. Here's the way I look at it: I'm eighteen, I haven't been around for a long, long time, and there's a lot of things to do out there. I don't plan to get married until I'm about twenty-six, twenty-seven, twenty-eight years old. That seems about the right time for me to take the plunge. Why put limits on yourself when you can meet more people? Right now, when I meet a girl and I date her, there's a lot of scrutiny and people are always looking to spread rumors. It takes a pretty strong person to go through all that stuff. The longest I've gone out with someone so far is six months. I'm not looking to settle down. I don't feel that I have to be in a relationship all the time to be happy. It's fun being single. I enjoy people who aren't afraid to stick up for themselves, who can see through phoniness. There are so many qualities you look for in the ideal partner.

I spend a lot of time thinking about what it will be like to be a father, about how my Dad reacts to situations and how hard it is. At the right time, I want to get married and have a family. I think it would be nice to have two or three kids.

Trusting people is not something that comes easily to me. To be quite frank, I haven't got a lot of friends because of that. For me, there's got to be trust built into the relationship. I trust my family totally, 100 percent, and I trust my close friends and my teammates. But once you've been burned a few times, you become very wary of people's motives.

When I was in my first year at Oshawa, I was paid an appearance fee to show up at a card show in Toronto. I had never done anything like that. It was arranged by my agent, Rick Curran, with the man who was running the show. I showed up and did my thing and even tried to help the guy out by giving him a stack of Durham Police hockey cards that he could hand out free to the people who were in line to get things signed. Well, to my surprise, this fellow stood at the beginning of the line and sold the cards to fans as they were coming through. The next thing I know, there's a story in the newspaper saying I'm selling my autograph to kids. That really hurt me; I felt I'd really been violated. The newspaper didn't even get my side of the story before they printed the article. The guy running the show later apologized and donated $500 to the Ontario Minor Hockey Association because of the incident, but the damage had already been done. That opened up my eyes totally to the business side and the media side of sports. A lot of people have tried to make money from my name, to take advantage of me for their own benefit. You feel at times as if everyone is trying to pull you in a certain direction.

That's not to say that being in the limelight doesn't have its share of perks. There are some neat opportunities that come your way. The Toronto Blue Jays let me take batting practice with them the summer after we won the Memorial Cup. I got to put the uniform on in the big-league clubhouse. I sat right beside the catcher, Pat Borders, down from Tom Henke and directly parallel to Dave Stieb. They had a bigger fridge full of beer, juice and pop than I've ever seen in my life. They had beer from Bora Bora. I was quiet; I didn't know what to say. The players thought I was there for a tryout and were asking where I was from.

"Toronto," I'd say.

"Toronto, Canada?"

Some of the players asked, "Are you a draft pick?"

When I got up to the plate, they quickly realized I wasn't a blue-chip prospect. I used Rance Mulliniks's bat, and I didn't do too badly considering I've only played on two school teams and one house league team in my entire life. But I don't claim to be a great ballplayer. The whole thing turned into a bit of a media circus. The manager, Cito Gaston, arrived on the scene to check me out. He was bigger than I ever dreamed he was. And he offered a pretty clear assessment of my potential in pro baseball.

"Well, son," he said, "good luck in hockey."

At home, everything is kept very low-key. I'm just a normal kid doing the dishes and cleaning my room. I don't like having to keep my guard up all the time. I usually go out with my friends a lot and hang out at their houses, because they treat me just like one of the guys. My really good friends understand the situation and know I don't like being in the public eye all the time. I'll go play some baseball with my friends Jeff Hardy and Lisa Best, or take off somewhere with my buddies Shannon Finn or Pete Bell. I don't like to stay around the rink, because they're always talking about hockey there. That can get boring after a while; you can only take so much. My friends and I will go grab some nachos somewhere or head for the bowling alley. I'm a horrible bowler, but I have fun and that's all that matters. I hit about 150 once, but it's pretty rare that I crack the 100 mark.

When I go out with my friends, they don't introduce me as a hockey player, they introduce me as a person. They don't treat me like I'm some big wheel, which I'm not. I'm just a regular kid who does something on the ice a little better than some other people. My friends let me have it if they think I'm getting a big head. They'll say, "Oh Eric, c'mon in the door. Oh, watch it, watch it, watch the doorway. Watch the doorway. Make sure you turn your head the right way to get in here." They do that stuff all the time. I'll say, "What did I do this time?" And the response will be, "Well, you think you're pretty good today." They cut me down and they keep me straight.

OTHER VOICES:

Pete Bell
(Eric's friend)

When we first got to know each other four years ago in cottage country, I knew that Eric was a hockey player, but we spent nearly every day together and he never once mentioned hockey.

At the cottage, hockey's far away, and he's just another kid having a great summer. When we're out, he often gets asked for his autograph, but he takes it all in stride. It sometimes spoils his evening a little bit. He starts off with the element of anonymity, but it sort of tones him down once he's recognized.

I'll arrive with him at a party and you can hear the murmurs starting. By the time I've hit the kitchen, about two minutes after we've walked in the door, the word's already out that "Eric Lindros is here." A lot of people who wouldn't give him the time of day before he was a hockey star now say, "Eric, buddy, I haven't seen you in so long." He takes it very well, but I would get frustrated and sort of think to myself, "These people aren't my friends. Why are they acting like they really are?" We went to a dance once and all kinds of people were shaking his hand and asking him how things were going. As we left, he said to me, "The last three people I spoke to never talked to me once the three years I went to the school." We just laughed about it for a minute or two. He seems on edge every once in a while when he meets a new person, because he's not quite sure what they're looking for.

OTHER VOICES:

Gil Hughes
(Eric's billet in Oshawa)

It was like Grand Central Station when Eric stayed at our place while he was with the Oshawa Generals. We had a steady stream of kids coming to the door for autographs at all times of the day. Cars would pull up to the driveway and a mother would open the door and four or five kids would pile out. Often the kids didn't have just one card—they had a whole stack they wanted signed. After a while, we had to put a halt to it and tell the kids to go down to the arena to get his autograph after a practice or a game, but some of those same kids would be back the next day trying it all over again.

Then there were the girls. Once word got out about where he was staying, they started calling at all hours of the night. I knew they weren't calling for me. Some of them would start crying when you told them he couldn't come to the phone.

The first year he stayed with us, a woman we knew asked if we could get him to go to her boy's birthday party. I mentioned it to Eric and, being the type of guy who just can't say no, he said he would drop by after practice. But this was during the playoffs, and the schedule was changed so that the Generals had a playoff game on the day of the birthday. I took it for granted that this lady would recognize the fact Eric had a hockey game that night and wouldn't be able to make it, but she called the next morning and blasted my wife for being inconsiderate. Eric tries to accommodate everybody, but I think he's found that it doesn't always work.

I would try to tell people he had to have some privacy; he's not a machine who doesn't have feelings. That was something that people couldn't seem to realize. I think if I were in his position I would be a little standoffish at times in order to get some space. I've been out with him in restaurants and they always seem to find his table. If you're eating your soup, you don't want somebody standing over you.

Eric's got a helluva lot on his plate, but he's a very smart, very calculating boy. There's not too much that goes by him. I've been amazed at how he reads situations, particularly off the ice. How many eighteen-year-old boys could do that? He's a very decent young man. I think Bonnie and Carl have given him a good upbringing that will remain with him the rest of his life. I don't think his head will ever get too big for his hockey helmet, because Carl and Bonnie are the type of people who will bring him down to earth in an awful hurry.

Larry Marson
(assistant coach, Oshawa Generals)

Eric was always willing to sign autographs after a game, but one night in Ottawa he wasn't feeling too good about himself because he had played what he considered a bad game. So he just signed a few autographs and then got on the team bus. The fans started chanting in some kind of singsong: "Eric's not a Gretzky . . . Eric's not a Gretzky." After a few minutes of that, he said "Forget this" and got off the bus to spend another half an hour signing autographs. In a lot of arenas, the same people who would boo and curse him all night would be the first ones in line for his autograph after the game was over. I used to get chuckles out of that.

There are times, though, when I get worried for him and I get scared for him, because to us, as outsiders, the whole thing he has to deal with just seems so big. But I have no qualms about his being able to deal with it, because of the type of person he is. To hear people like Bobby Orr or Gordie Howe make comments about how he handles himself so well is a credit to Eric and his family. But for an eighteen-year-old kid, I just wonder sometimes when he goes home at night if he sits there and thinks, "Can I handle all this?"

━━━━━━━━━

Sometimes I feel like a bird on a wire with two strings around my neck—or three strings, or four strings, or a million strings. And people are pulling me everywhere. There are so many power struggles. People want you to do this; people want you to do that. But they don't understand that I'm not a bird on a wire. I'm there for life. I'll be on that wire for life. And it doesn't matter how hard they pull, because I'm the strongest bird and I'm not budging. I can learn and understand and take note of what they're saying and pick out the good stuff and sort through it. I can lean very far—but they can't pull me off.

10

Graduation Day

"Les Nordiques de Québec . . . select as first pick overall in the 1991 NHL annual draft . . . from the Oshawa Generals of the OHL, Eric Lindros."

The announcement by Pierre Pagé lasted only twenty-six seconds, but to me it seemed to take forever for the Quebec Nordiques general manager to get the words out. The Nordiques knew I didn't want to play for them and, although the chances were pretty slim, I was hoping for an announcement of a different kind to kick off the draft—that Quebec had traded the number one pick.

It was a tense wait in the stands with my family at the Memorial Auditorium in Buffalo. We were sitting among other junior players and their families who had come from all over for the National Hockey League draft in June 1991. The place was jammed with more than thirteen thousand hockey fans; it almost felt like a playoff game. Most of the players were nervous because they didn't know what was going to happen. I already knew what was going to happen, I was just nervous about what was going to happen afterwards. The other players were finally going to learn where they'd begin their pro careers, but I couldn't share their sense of anticipation. I knew I'd still be in the same place at the end of the day—limbo.

Everything happened so fast after the Nordiques announced my name. It's all a bunch of blurred images now—walking to the podium, the cameras clicking away, being hustled from interview to interview, reporters firing off question after question. It was like a mirage of people—they were there, but they weren't really there, because I wasn't really focused. I brought my brother Brett with me everywhere. I felt secure with him there. It was hectic, but I held myself together through it all. I was smiling on the outside.

I had been dreaming of draft day for as long as I could remember, but when it finally came, it left me feeling so empty. I felt great satisfaction in knowing that I had been the first player selected overall in the 1991 NHL Entry Draft. But at the same time, I was upset that the first pick wasn't the happiest player— not even close. Knowing that things could never work out with the Quebec Nordiques took a lot of the joy out of the day.

When all the interviews were over, I went back to sit in the stands with my family. I was still wishing that Brian O'Neill, the NHL executive vice-president who was conducting the draft, would announce that the Nordiques had traded my rights. Deep down, though, I knew it wouldn't happen.

I took a lot of flak for not putting the Nordiques sweater on, but I think wearing the sweater would have been a false statement. I didn't want to misguide people as to my true feelings, particularly anyone from the Quebec organization.

My parents threw a party for me at a hotel in Buffalo that afternoon, and many of my relatives and friends were there. There was a big cake with a design of me in a Team Canada uniform on the top and a friend showed up with a new set of golf clubs for me. It was a good chance for me to forget about everything for a while. We had a putting competition, complete with commentary, and a couple of my friends made their exits moonwalking backwards into the hotel fountain. Everything should have been great, but I still didn't feel right. I don't want to say I was putting on a show, but everyone knew that I wasn't really happy.

In the early evening, when the draft was over, I went back to the arena by myself. I walked out onto the main floor among the NHL teams' abandoned draft tables and looked up at the big board displaying the team emblems and all the names of the players selected. It set in then: "Okay, the draft is over now. Here comes the hard part."

That night a group of us went out to celebrate. Some of the guys were players who got drafted, including Scott Lachance, picked fourth overall by the New York Islanders, and Steve Staios, who was selected by St. Louis early in the second round. Brad May, my friend and teammate from the world junior team, also came along; so did my brother Brett, and some of my cousins and friends. All the players drafted were wearing their new teams' NHL hats. It was like a graduation day. I was supposed to have graduated at the top of my class, but I didn't have my graduation hat on—and I yearned for that hat. All the guys knew I was upset and they kept lending me their hats. It was sort of a joke, but inside it felt good to put on a hat from a team that I might want to go to.

I kept a lid on my emotions until the end of the day. Then it hit me full force during the cab ride back to the hotel. I sat and cried in my brother's lap; I cried all the way back to the hotel. All Brett kept saying was, "Don't worry."

Brett Lindros

Draft day was more emotional than anything else for Eric. You've got to see different sides of my brother to understand him. He's basically a kid and he's got to deal with these grown men and they're trying to make him do this and that. I know he's handled it before, but these guys are big-time.

I was sitting with some of the other players' parents in the stands at the draft and, when their sons got picked, they got all excited. But when Eric's name was announced, we knew what was going to happen so we didn't really have the same feeling. I think Eric sort of got left out. Even though he was the best player available, it didn't work out for him.

Some of the media were unreal. These were a bunch of eighteen-year-old kids and these reporters were hanging off every word they said. Eric's been doing lots of interviews since he was fifteen or sixteen, but some of the other guys have only been interviewed by their local papers, and all of a sudden they have this horde of reporters sticking microphones in their faces. It can be overwhelming. I got really embarrassed when Eric hauled me up on the podium during a news conference after he got picked. That was pressure.

The press conference the day before the draft was unbelievable. You had Jean Perron, the former NHL coach who now works as a broadcaster covering the Nordiques, telling Eric he's going to break up Canada if he doesn't go to Quebec. Gimme a break! I think I would have lost it on some of the questions. Eric's a little more relaxed than he used to be, but it bothered me to see how they were trying to get to him. Most of the reporters were fine, but some of the Quebec guys were really trying to get the dirt.

On the morning of the draft, we got up at about ten, two hours before it started. We were so disorganized, we just threw our clothes on. When we got there it was pretty tense, so we started fooling around. Mike Torchia was sitting in his seat singing, and that got Eric relaxed. "Torch" was doing dances to keep Eric and himself loose, and it really helped. It was weird; everything happened so fast. The next thing I know I'm in front of all these microphones with Eric. One guy thought I was a prospect and nearly put me in an Upper Deck card. It was really hectic.

The morning after the draft, Eric was really depressed. I think it wouldn't have been as bad if he hadn't gone out with some of the other players after it was over. He saw how happy they were, and he's in this weird situation. It's really an odd position for an eighteen-year-old. I think it's hard on him. He tries to blow it off and pretend it doesn't matter, but that doesn't work on me.

I think Eric needs more people around him just to feel secure. He hauled me around with him everywhere at the draft. I think he needed me there, but again he tried to blow it off. "Well, they want to see you," he said. Sure.

OTHER VOICES:

Rick Curran
(Eric's agent)

What we had always hoped was that we could convince the Nordiques that the number one pick was an even more valuable asset than they had considered. If they had decided to auction off the pick, they might have found themselves over-compensated.

From a business standpoint, it would have made a lot of sense for them. They might have been able to obtain a quality forward, defenseman, draft picks and even money if they had handled it properly. But our meeting and discussions prior to the draft, where we presented this point of view, seemed to be ineffective and, if anything, fueled the fire. As things developed, the Nordiques became obsessed with drafting Eric, and logic was replaced with emotion. It was really frustrating to see the opportunity disappear.

Whether we're talking about Eric or about any client I represent, my job is to ensure that his net income is not adversely affected by where he happens to end up as an NHL player. There's no reason why Eric should find himself at an economic disadvantage because he was selected by the Nordiques, yet that's exactly what he was faced with. It seems unfair that, as a result of playing in Quebec City, Eric might make only 40 percent after taxes of what he could earn in many other NHL communities.

It quickly became clear to us that it was going to be nearly impossible for the Nordiques to come close to matching what Eric could earn elsewhere. If you look at the extra tax bite and particularly the loss of endorsement opportunities Eric would face by playing in Quebec City, you can see that it would cost the Nordiques twice as much to give him compensation equal to what he could make with a dozen other NHL teams. Eric already has an endorsement income exceeded by that of only half a dozen players in the NHL. He has the potential to earn at least as much from endorsement opportunities as from his hockey salary if he's playing in a major market. That net-income figure becomes almost prohibitive for any club to be able to pay. Can the Nordiques afford to compensate Eric and yet still maintain a competitive team around him, a competitive team still based in Quebec City? They might be able to afford him, but could they then afford anybody else? Hockey is not a one-man game. You have to question whether it's a feasible strategy for a hockey team located in such a limited location.

Eric is prepared to wait for the proper situation. Unfortunately for him, in the NHL, the draft shackles a player more than it does in any other major pro sport. Eric can't play professionally anywhere for two years if he wants the chance to enter the draft again, and even then, Quebec general manager Pierre Pagé suggested to me during one of our phone conversations that the Nordiques might come in last and once again pull the top draft pick. If Eric plays in another pro league or goes to Europe, his NHL rights would still belong to the Nordiques. But in the National Basketball Association and National Football League, a player has the chance to re-enter the draft after sitting out one year and becomes a total free agent after two years. In baseball, the rules are similar and, if a player were to sit out one year after getting drafted as a senior out of college, he would get total free agency and be able to negotiate with the team of his choice.

Some people suggested Eric should give the Nordiques a try and, if things didn't work, then move on elsewhere. But it's not that simple. How do you get out once you're in? Eric knew the trouble I was having this past summer trying to move my free agent clients to other teams. He realized free agency was a façade, and that the system would never let him leave, no matter how intolerable the situation might become.

Through spending time at my office, Eric is well aware that hockey owners treat their teams as a business, first and foremost. He's had a glimpse of what goes on with other players, how they can get bounced around from one team to another at a moment's notice and suddenly have to buy a new house and pull the kids out of school, or have to cope with injuries and various other setbacks. He knows very vividly what life can be like in the pros, and how short that life can be. It's important to be in a place where you can maximize your economic return, or to be so happy in all other regards that it's not so much of an issue.

Some people suggest that Eric is only interested in money, but they don't understand him. I've watched him turn down close to $400,000 over the past two years because he didn't believe in the projects that were being offered. He rejected a lucrative poster deal that would have netted him well over $100,000. He had agreed to do it if Oshawa advanced to the 1991 Memorial Cup. That way, most of the money could go to his teammates and their families, to help defray the costs of going to the Cup, and the balance would go to a charity. But when Oshawa was eliminated from the play-offs, he nixed the deal. Does that sound like a money-hungry kid?

I think Eric has come to grips with the fact that, no matter what he does or doesn't do, there will be people critical of him. We try to be very careful and selective in determining the ventures to pursue. We often hold a bull session to get everybody's views when it comes to big decisions. That's the beauty of having people like lawyer Gordon Kirke who has great judgment and is able to look at the big picture. You have Carl, who's very analytical and methodical. And you have Bonnie, who never lets us forget the person in Eric.

Bonnie Lindros

Eric has enough self-confidence to do what he thinks is right rather than following the crowd, which is often the easier way.

Our kids have a great sense of fairness. Eric knows what's fair and what's right, and he's willing to speak up about it. He wants to enter a situation that he feels will work for him, and he will do whatever he has to do to make sure that happens. He won't give up and he won't waver. No matter how gruelling or how tough something is, he won't quit.

Every parent's dream is for their kids to be healthy and happy. Eric has his reasons why he won't be happy in Quebec City, but for most kids the draft works out fine, and it would be unfair to think that would be the scenario for everybody.

Eric has worked very hard at school and he's worked very hard at hockey. He has achieved far beyond his dreams, and he wants to feel that there's a reward there for him. If he is put in a place where the plus side is very short for him and the minus side is very long, then that isn't a reward for him, and he will not choose that route.

We never gave the kids presents if they did well in school. With all three of them, we wanted the reward to be the feeling that they would get inside from having done a good job, a feeling of being content and comfortable with themselves. To work that hard in hockey and not feel comfortable with what happened to him is hard for Eric to accept.

Whatever route he decides to go, he will put his whole heart into it, and whatever team and organization happen to get him will be the beneficiaries. Eric doesn't like bucking the tide, he doesn't want to be a crusader. But everyone wants to be allowed to have some say in the direction of his life.

OTHER VOICES:

Carl Lindros

The days and weeks leading up to the draft were pretty nerve-wracking for all of us. We were hoping that the Nordiques would recognize that things weren't going to work out with Eric, and that they would trade their pick. But in retrospect, particularly considering that the NHL rules prevent any serious discussions prior to the draft, I can see why Nordiques president Marcel Aubut would draft him and then meet with us before deciding whether or not to make a trade. That's only good business. We're hopeful we can eventually reach an understanding and something can be worked out that's in everyone's best interests.

One of the things we hoped for is that wherever Eric played hockey he would have an opportunity to get involved in the business aspect of that team, or with one of its related companies, so that he would be learning skills useful after hockey. Is that likely to work as well for Eric in Quebec City as it would elsewhere? Because of the language situation and the size of the community, his options are dramatically fewer than they would be almost anywhere else in the NHL. The other thought was that Eric would try to attend a university to take one course while he's playing. It would give Eric an opportunity to think about something other than hockey and to associate with students his own age. But that outlet isn't there because there are no English-language universities in Quebec City.

The political situation is something that also really worries us. As we understand it, Quebec City is a hotbed of the separatist movement. If it comes down to a referendum, a Nordique who's strongly against separatism isn't going to be the most popular man in town. If Eric says that he thinks Quebec should be an integral and desirable part of Canada, a contributing member of the most important Canadian team—which is the way he feels—I think there could be a tremendous backlash from perhaps as many as 65 to 70 percent of the fans in Quebec City, at least as I read the stats in the newspapers. What happens if you're trying to play hockey and suddenly you're lambasted by the fans because of your political views? If you know there's a strong likelihood of that situation happening, why begin? Eric has played for his country on three national teams. It would be difficult for him to play in a city that would like to separate from the rest of Canada.

One also has to think about Eric's other options. You're only young once, why rush it? Would it be better for Eric to play in a less competitive environment for a while to further refine his skills, as Gretzky and Messier did at roughly his age? What about the opportunity of playing for your country in the Olympics and learning the game from Dave King?

There's a lot of pain and agony and anguish and anxiety that goes along with sticking up for what you think is right. Eric's been through a lot of battles. But most of the time, when you go through a battle, you end up a better individual for having gone through it, whether you win or lose. You learn something from it.

We haven't made playing in the NHL the be-all and end-all for Eric. If it doesn't happen for a while, that's fine. If it doesn't happen at all, that's unfortunate. I know that would be a very sad event in Eric's life, but he might be prepared for it.

One of the big concerns as we look into the future is how happy Eric will be. How satisfied will he be when he's fifty-five? In life, the final report card starts to become clear, I think, by the time you're going into your early fifties. A lot of today's events are just slices of life. Eric right now is getting closer and closer to the pinnacle of athletic success. Let's suppose he does very well in the NHL within a few years. In a sense, from a professional hockey perspective, he may peak by the time he is twenty-one. Well, you've got a whole life ahead of you. What's going to drive you? What's going to give you satisfaction? What's going to give your life meaning and richness? What's going to keep it moving, so that by the time you're fifty-five, you can say, "I made good use of it. I was very lucky. I feel happy. I feel satisfied. I've got this contentment"? The challenges of hockey and the challenges that he's been through to date may be nothing compared to the challenge that's going to be ahead of him in terms of what's really important.

My family has backed me from day one. The way I see it, you're only as good as your family. I'm a product of the values my parents instilled in me.

I was raised to believe in hard work, because if you worked hard—at school, at sports, at your job—you'd have more choices. Give it everything you've got, strive to achieve, and all the doors will be open to you. The harder you worked, the more options you'd have. It seemed so simple and it seemed so true, and I still believe it's right. That's the reason I want some say in my own future.

Once I thought about all the other options, I knew I wasn't likely ever to sign with the Quebec Nordiques. I've been to Quebec City—it's a nice place and has terrific hockey fans—but I've thought long and hard about it and I know that I couldn't live there. It's a combination of things: part of it is economics, part of it is the political situation and all the related issues and tensions and part of it is my perception of the track record of the Quebec Nordiques' organization. Why go into a situation where you know you're not going to be happy? Why try to force some-one to live in an environment when it's going to affect his game and the entire team? I want to live in a place where I feel comfort-able, where I feel that I can establish roots and where I might be able to settle down after I'm finished with hockey.

A lot of people are going to look at the situation and say, "The kid's so selfish. He should be giving Quebec a try." But the easy way out would be to sign the big ticket with the Nordiques. And all I'd be doing is robbing people. If I'm not happy, I'm not going to play well. What's the point of going to a position where you get all this money and you're not going to be happy? Why not wait and learn more and be happy within? Money's not every-thing. It can wait. Everyone wants to be paid what they feel they're worth, but it's just as important to feel right about what you're doing.

I never take things lying down. It's just the way I am. If you take things lying down, that's when you get stomped on. I feel secure inside that I'm doing what's best for me.

I'm prepared to go back to junior hockey if I have to, and wait two years and re-enter the draft. There's still a lot for me to learn about hockey. In two years, I'll be twenty. A lot of players don't even get out of the minors until they're twenty-two. So, I'll be two years ahead of them. I'll have that much more school and I'll be that much closer to having a degree and throwing it in my back pocket and showing it can be done. I can learn new things, not only about life but about hockey as well. I would be able to spend more time with my family and friends if I were playing in Oshawa again. I was ready to leave junior hockey behind, but it can't be that bad when the people there want you and you're happy to go there.

I spent this past summer working hard to get ready to make the team for the Canada Cup. I was really focused on that. After that, I'm focused to return to Oshawa to play for the Generals,

en to the world juniors and then to the Olympics. Then, the
cus is on the Memorial Cup.

Life has ups and downs. To feel successful within yourself
nd to be confident and secure, sometimes you have to hold out
r a little while and ride the downs before the ups can happen.
nd when the ups start happening, they'll just wash out the
owns, totally. That's the way that I perceive it. Everything's
oing to work out.

I won't kid you, I'm dying for the chance to play in the NHL. I
ve the game of hockey and I want to play it at the highest level.
hings have certainly changed since my days on the backyard
nk, when my biggest concern was how to negotiate an extra ten
inutes on the ice. Hockey's a different game for me now. My
rst love was the total freedom it gave me. Now, it's my career;
's not a hobby anymore. But it's a great career.

I just want to go somewhere where I can perform and be one
f the key members of the team. I want to help raise a team's abil-
y and stature and help make it win. I don't want to be looked at
s the *one* player who's supposed to make a team win; you need a
umber of people to make a team win. More than anything, I
ant to play on a winner. Forget points and all that stuff; that's
ne, but those are secondary goals. To me, the real players are
layers who win, who are on teams that win. It's fine to score
oals, but when you win the scoring title your team doesn't
ways win the Cup.

I'm sure I'm going to be a target in the pros, both for the other
layers and the press. I'm not saying I deserve it, but I'm the new
d on the block. They're going to take their runs at me. I'm not
o worried about handling myself on the ice, but it's going to be
lot tougher than it was in junior hockey. Okay, say they beat me
p the first two years. Hopefully, they're still playing by my third
ar, because what goes around, comes around, and I'm sure I'll
e stronger by then.

The initiation period will take place within the team first. I was the same when I joined Oshawa. The guys were really good but they didn't accept me right from the start. It's a fact of life. It's a job now, a business, and I'm going to be taking someone else's job. Someone's going to be out of work or get traded, and I'm not exactly going to be welcomed with open arms. But I'll be ready—it's been that way all the way up.

I just want to get the respect of my teammates. That comes from the way you carry yourself, your attitude about the game and making sure you stand up for your team. If someone runs our goalie, then I'll choose my time to even the score. If I get my butt kicked, fine, but at least I'll have shown the other players that I'm not going to back down.

At the end of my hockey career, I'd like to be able to say that was the best I could possibly be, and that I made a lot of really good friends I'll have for the rest of my life. I'm looking for security in friends who I can really, really trust. It would also be nice to have enough money to help out someone else. So far, everything has been done to help me. I want to be able to help my brother, my sister, my parents and my community.

There's been a lot of speculation, but I don't think anyone—including me—knows how good I'm going to be. Since I was fifteen years old playing for St. Mike's in Junior B, people have been saying that I'm going to be hockey's next franchise player. They seem to want to categorize me—"the Next Gretzky," "the Next Lemieux," "the Next One." It's a great honor to be compared to those players, but it's not me.

I'd rather be known as an up and coming player. I'll get my time, I'll get my chance to shine, I know I will. I've just got to be patient, trained, ready and confident. A lot of people come to see me play expecting a certain thing, but I don't play like anyone else, really. Physically, I'm like some players. Size-wise I'm like some players. Seeing the ice, I'm like some players

Skating, I'm like some players. But no two players are identical.

It's not that I mind the comparisons, but it's good and bad, because a lot of people don't understand. I don't proclaim to be better than anyone else; I'm different from everyone else. I don't want to be a clone. All I want to be is myself.

11

A Boy Among Men

I had to look twice at my reflection in the glass over the boards at Maple Leaf Gardens—and even then I could hardly believe where I was. But, sure enough, that was my face staring back at me, and all I could think was, "Wow, here I am!"

I was on the ice for Team Canada's opening practice for the 1991 Canada Cup. I was in awe, and more than a little nervous. I don't think I said a word in the dressing room before we went on the ice.

I was prepared to do whatever it would take to earn one of those Team Canada sweaters, but the competition was going to be fierce. There were sixty guys there, and everybody wanted a job—badly.

I had an idea of what was expected of me. The night I arrived, I spoke with Mike Keenan, the head coach and general manager of Team Canada. He gave me a bit of a pep talk. He told me, "You possess certain skills and you have to use those skills to be the best you can be. Do that and you'll be fine. I don't know if you have a job, because no one has a job. The only guy who has a job for sure is Gretzky. I don't know if Coffey has a job. Messier's not here so we're looking for a power center. Go and do your best."

My attitude from the opening scrimmage was "I'm here to get a job. I'm here to steal a job. I'm going to go out hitting." It was "bump and be bumped." I realized that's what I had to do to try to make the team. It was also the way I had to play to create some room for myself.

I had trouble shooting the puck in the warm-up. Kids in peewee hockey fire the puck harder than I was shooting it that day. It was just nerves. Once we got into the game, I started hitting and I felt okay.

On the first shift of the intra-squad game, I ran over Calgary defenseman Al MacInnis and I thought, "Did I really just knock over Al MacInnis? He's a Norris Trophy winner!"

I also found myself on a collision course with Luc Robitaille, a high-scoring forward with the Los Angeles Kings. On one play, we were both chasing the puck into the corner. He tried to hit me, but I was moving in at full speed to hit him, and I caught him with a pretty good check. His helmet went spinning on the ice. We ended up coming back to the bench at the same time, and Luc took a pretty good ribbing from his teammates on the blue team.

"Nice hit, Luc!"

"Way to take the body, Luc!"

Here's a fifty-goal scorer from the NHL and we're out there competing against each other. I loved it!

After the first day, Wayne Gretzky was talking with a mutual friend about my chances of sticking with the team, and Wayne said, "The kid's going to make it." My friend told me that, and then my confidence just went soaring!

But I never took it for granted that I would make the team. In fact, I was always worried about getting cut. I hung out mostly with some of the younger guys on the team, like Brendan Shanahan, who had just signed with St. Louis after playing out his option in New Jersey, and Shayne Corson of the Montreal Canadiens. We seemed to be able to relate to each other pretty well and had a lot of fun together. Like me, they were both trying to make their first Canada Cup team. We were all quite nervous.

Dale Hawerchuk, a veteran center with Buffalo who had plenty of Canada Cup experience, was always trying to calm me down. I often sat near him on the bus that took us back and forth from our charter flights. I'd be saying, "I hope I got a spot . . . I hope I got a spot." He'd be saying, "Relax, you're sure to have made this team. You came and you did a good job. Don't worry about it. You've got to have a spot." That gave me a lot of confidence.

I was eager to please and made sure I was always out on the ice pretty early for practice. Gretzky was usually one of the first guys out there. He'd be skating around, and if he looked like he needed a puck, my attitude was, "I'd better get him a puck!" I was sort of intimidated.

I roomed with New York Rangers veteran Mike Gartner at the start, but then he hurt his knee and had to leave training camp. He was an unbelievably great guy. He's very goal-oriented. He'd wake up in the morning and he'd read the Bible for a little bit, and then, whether it was raining or sunny outside, he'd say, "What a great day! We sure are lucky!" It really brought you up a little bit hearing all this. We would talk about how we were enjoying training camp and how we could get better. I'd hear him talking to his kids on the phone and you just knew he'd be a great dad. "How you doin', sport?" he'd say to his son on the phone. I felt great listening to him.

Another player who really treated me well was Steve Yzerman. There was a lot of talk early in training camp about the Quebec

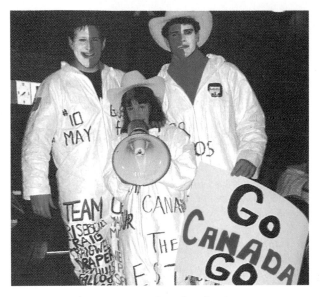

Let's Go Canada! Team Canada's cheerleading corps in Saskatoon—Brad May's brother Darryl (left), Robin and Brett.

All together now. Belting out the national anthem after beating the Soviets for the gold medal at the 1991 World Junior Championships in Saskatoon. What a feeling! (Photo couresy of Claus Anderson/ALLSPORT)

Left: An unruly crowd gets on my case during the Ontario Hockey League final in Sault Ste. Marie, 1991. (Photo by Ken Faught, courtesy of *The Toronto Star*)

Right: We're Number One. Celebrating with "Big Carl" after we won the gold medal at the world juniors in Saskatoon. (Photo courtesy of Claus Anderson/ ALLSPORT)

Right: Golden double. As a member of Canada's national junior squad, I was fortunate to play on teams that won back-to-back gold medals at the World Junior Championships. (Photo by Ron Vesely, courtesy of Score hockey cards)

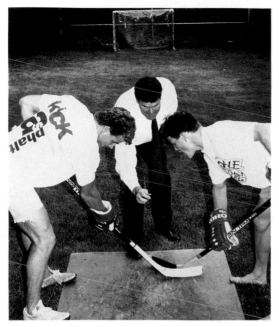

Dad plays referee as Brett and I face off. (Photo by Ron Vesely, courtesy of Score hockey cards)

A little relaxation at the end of a long day. Celebrating with family and friends after the National Hockey League Draft. (Photo by Peter Power, courtesy of *The Toronto Star*)

Above: Another season in Oshawa? (Photo by Al Gilbert)

Above: Reflecting at the end o a long day. The opening day training camp for the 1991 Canada Cup gave me a little taste of what was to become great experience. (Photo by Keith Beaty, courtesy of *The Toronto Star*)

Left: In the eye of the storm. I took a lot of heat leading up t the game against the Soviets during the Canada Cup. (Photo by Tony Bock, courtesy of *The Toronto Star*)

The thrill of victory. Celebrating with (from left to right) Shayne Corson, Russ Courtnall and Luc Robitaille after winning the Canada Cup. (Photo courtesy of Claus Anderson/ALLSPORT)

"Goin' for the gold." Playing in the Olympics was a really good experience. (Photo courtesy of Claus Anderson/ALLSPORT)

I lived with our goaltender, Sean Burke, at the Olympic team's home base in Calgary. "Burkie" is a great guy and one of the main reasons we won a silver medal. (Photo courtesy of Claus Anderson/ALLSPORT)

Whoa! What a relief! Dave Tippett (left) and Dave Hannan (right) congratulate me after scoring in the sudden-death shoot-out against the Germans. (Photo by Gary Hershorn/Reuters)

Silver lining. I really wanted to hear the Canadian anthem played at the end of the Olympic hockey tournament. (Photo by Bonnie Lindros)

A moment I'll never forget. Accepting the silver medal after the Olympic final in Meribel France. (Photo by Ryan Remiorz/ Canapress)

Helping Gordie celebrate his 64th birthday at the Sports Federation of Canada banquet after the Olympic Games. I was presented with the Viscount Alexander Trophy as Canada's Top Junior Male Athlete. (Photo by Norm Betts/*The Toronto Sun*)

Pondering the future. (Photo by Rick Chard/Canapress)

Nordiques trading me to the Detroit Red Wings for Yzerman. It could have been an uncomfortable situation, but Steve is a classy guy. He was always rooting for me to play better. I remember we were in Montreal for a pre-season game and I was playing really well. After the second period I had a pair of goals, and Steve told me in the dressing room, "Keep going, kid. Don't stop at two. Go for the third." He was always supportive.

I remember the night we went to play in Detroit. Of course the Red Wings fans cheered Steve while I got the raspberries. Steve was really good about it, though. After they booed me, he just looked over at me and said, "Don't worry, it's just my family."

I performed well in the pre-tournament games, but not everything went smoothly. In one of the early games, in Ottawa, they staged a shoot-out for the fans between the first and second periods. The fans had been getting on my case during the game, as they did in junior. I figured the shoot-out would be a good chance to silence some of the critics.

I had to shoot second and they had just flooded the ice. The first shooter had gone in on the side because the ice was dry there, but in a stroke of brilliance I decided to go right down the middle where it was still pretty wet. Here I am, shaking in my skates as I move in on the goaltender, and the puck is sticking to the ice! I was shoveling the puck towards the net and I barely got a shot away. I think the goalie had enough time to get two pads and a glove on it! Pat Burns, one of our assistant coaches and head coach of the Montreal Canadiens, was on the other bench, and he was just laughing his head off and really giving it to me.

Burns is an intense guy, but he can be a lot of fun. He really went out of his way to help me. If I had any questions about defensive coverage, he would fill me in. I was asking a lot of questions, even while the scrimmages were going on. I'm sure the guys on the bench were thinking, "What is this kid doing? Why is he asking all these questions? Who cares? Let's just play hockey."

Burns and I had had a pretty interesting introduction. I was going up on the elevator with him on the second day of training camp and he just gave me a look. It wasn't a cold look, but then again it wasn't warm, either. And then he spoke to me.

"I really think you should go to Quebec."

I think he was just trying to see what kind of reaction he could get out of me. The Nordiques are the Canadiens' hated division rivals, so Burns and I would be seeing a lot of each other if I were to take his advice. But I knew then that there was no way I was ever going to be suiting up for the Nordiques.

"I don't think that's ever going to happen," I told him.

Burns looked at me deadpan and just shrugged his shoulders.

"Well, if you don't go, it's not going to hurt me, because I don't *want* to see you eight times a year."

We both laughed. We got along really well after that.

The coaches worked us hard right from day one of training camp. Sometimes you couldn't feel your legs at the end of a long day. I remember we were doing a skating drill at the close of one practice to get into shape. We had to pick up the pace every time Mike Keenan blew the whistle. Keenan's a fitness nut, and I think that's good. It really helped the team. But on this day, I was especially worn out. And it seemed no matter which way I turned, the coaches were picking on me.

Pat Burns said something to me. I turned around and gave him a bit of a look. Shayne Corson, who plays under Burns in Montreal, was skating with me and knew right away I'd made the wrong move. Burns started yelling at me: "What the hell are you looking at? What the hell are you looking at?" Corson told me, "Turn your head and start skatin'! Shut up, Eric, just start skatin'!"

I didn't say a word. I knew I'd better take his advice. I just put my head down and skated as fast as I could.

Even though the battle for spots was pretty heated, there was a lot of camaraderie in the dressing room. Wendel Clark of the

Leafs was a great guy. One night at dinner someone asked him what he thought he was going to do after hockey. He said, "I think I'll go back to the farm. You come to the rink, you work hard—I'll put in my time and then I'll head back to the farm."

After weeks of blood and sweat, D-day finally came. I remember Shanahan and I were in the dressing room when the official 1991 Team Canada lineup went up on the board. We took a deep breath before stepping up to take a look. Shanny's name was on the board . . . Corson's name was on the board . . . *my* name was on the board! Shanny and I just looked at one another with massive grins. We sat down beside each other on the bench and I whispered to him.

"Can you believe this? Can you *believe* this? This is unbelievable!"

He was just as excited as I was. We were really pumped. But we sat there and tried to act nonchalant. We were strolling around the dressing room like there was nothing to it.

Shanahan and I had developed a routine of whistling to each other whenever we got really excited. We wound up doing that a lot before games. Before the first game, we were both really nervous. It was in Toronto, which was hometown for both of us, and we were thinking, "I can't believe I'm here!" So we'd whistle— kind of like, "Ho-hum, oh, we're in the Canada Cup. There's Wayne Gretzky, there's Mark Messier doing his sticks." And we'd whistle like it was nothing. When we'd get really nervous, one guy would notice the other guy and he'd catch his eye and start whistling to loosen him up a little bit. I don't think anybody else noticed it; we just quietly whistled away.

All the hard work I had done over the summer paid off. Usually, I don't put the blades on until a week before training camp. This year, I had them on early because I had to do my homework. Along with weight lifting, for four weeks I spent three days each week on the ice with my brother Brett and coach Dan Cameron, who had helped me out in Junior B hockey. We worked on everything—tactics, connecting on one-timers, quick starts, exploding on impact when you hit. It was pretty feisty at times. I know I came home a couple days with black eyes, and so did Brett. Brett is really starting to come into his own as a hockey player, and it's fun to see.

A lot of great players got cut. Steve Yzerman didn't even make the starting lineup for the opening game and eventually left. The competition for jobs was that wicked. I think our intra-squad games were played as hard as Stanley Cup playoff battles. Players were putting up brave fronts during the practices, but it really took a physical toll. They'd get back to their rooms and they'd tell their roommates, "Man, am I hurting!"

Gary Roberts of the Calgary Flames really impressed me. He'll hit, he'll get in your face, he can fight if he has to, he can score, he can skate, and he's a good team guy. But when Mark Messier joined the team near the end of training camp, Roberts wound up being the odd man out. When you're cutting guys like him, then you know you've got one heck of a team.

I think my role changed, too, after Messier came. Messier had been recovering from some injuries and it didn't look like he'd be available until the last minute. Keenan had been looking for someone to fill the position of power center and now he had the best in the business. I was sitting around the dressing room the day Messier arrived.

"How ya doin', kid?" he said. "Good to meet ya. Let's get busy."

I walked by our starting goaltender, Bill Ranford, who played with Messier in Edmonton, and he said, "Well, there he is. There's our fearless leader."

Fearless doesn't begin to describe Messier. He's not only fearless, he's downright scary. When he has something to do, he just goes out and gets the job done. He has the right attitude: Work hard, play hard. Whatever he sets out to do, he does it well.

I really admire Messier as a player. I'd like to develop a lot of the qualities he has on the ice. I like the way he's able to shoot off the wrong wing. I'd like to have the mental edge that he has. I tried to learn as much as I could from him during the Canada Cup. I'd watch the way he skated around in the warm-up. He'd get that intense stare going, and I'd try to get a stare going too. I would watch everything he did.

Messier's a great guy. I roomed with him a couple of times near the end of the tournament in Hamilton. He was a riot!

I talked to Bill Ranford about moves more than anyone else. I was telegraphing some of my shots—you could tell what I was going to do a mile away. Bill Ranford told me he would work with me on it after practice one day. We worked for a good half hour. After that, I started shooting the puck harder and better and more accurately. Ranford was unbelievable in goal for us during the tournament. I don't know if he has a house big enough for all the appliances he won as our MVP in game after game. I think he wound up with a whole stereo system!

The depth of the team was incredible. If you didn't have Billy Ranford in goal, you had Ed Belfour, who'd won the Calder and Vezina trophies as the best rookie and goaltender in the NHL the previous year. And if you didn't have Belfour, you had Sean Burke, who went on to play amazingly in the Olympics. It kind of puts things in perspective.

I thought it would be hard being so much younger than any of the other players, but it was never really a problem. I never felt left out or out of place. The guys really made me feel part of the team, and always made sure to include me in things. Eddie Belfour was a really funny guy. He loves cars and he was always looking at car magazines. He hung around a lot with Steve Larmer, whom we called "Larms," and Dirk (Duke) Graham, since they were all on the Chicago Blackhawks together. Eddie knew that I love cars too, so he would always be saying to me,

"Well, what do you think about this car, kid?" And then he would ask Larms. Eddie always loved the car, and Larms always said he hated it. And then Eddie would say, "What do you know, Steve? You drive a truck!"

One night Brendan Shanahan and I were out for the night with Larms. Shanahan and I were dressed really casually—we had our blue jeans on, running shoes and T-shirts. Larmer looked at Shanny and me and said, "Look at you guys. You're both bums. Look at ya, you're bums. . . . Cheers! Never change!" He was just like that. He's a quiet guy, always chewing gum. And can he ever play the game. He's as good on offense as he is on defense. He does a great job backchecking.

The player who impressed me the most physically was one of our defensemen, Scott Stevens. Scott looks like Jean Claude Van Damme, the martial arts fighter from action movies like *Double Impact* and *Universal Soldier*. You should have seen him. Wow! He's just huge. He blew everybody away in the physical fitness testing on the opening day of training camp.

Brent Sutter, who was still a member of the New York Islanders at the time, was my roommate right after the team was picked in Toronto. I'm superstitious, so I always try to take the bed on the left side of the room. But Sutter threw all his stuff on the left bed. As we were getting ready to go to sleep, I asked about making a switch.

"Are you going to take that bed?"

"Why?" asked Sutter.

"I always sort of sleep on the left bed."

"Kid, I've been in this league for twelve years," said Sutter. "I always have the left bed. You haven't even been in the league yet. I think the right will do you fine."

I wasn't about to argue with that, especially since he'd said it in a good-natured way. He's a great guy. He talked with me about all the abuse my mother was taking in the press at the time. It was really starting to bother me. He told me, "Your mother's just being like any other mother. She's being protective. She loves you so much that she's putting her neck on the line. My Mom would do the same thing for me or any of my brothers. The only difference is your Mom's got press about it. My Mom's done the same thing for me, day in, day out. You should be proud." It was a big deal to me that he would say that. I really appreciated it.

I think the reason my Mom was getting so much press was part of a Nordique strategy to belittle her. On the one hand Marcel Aubut says he doesn't understand why there should be any hard feelings between my Mom and him since they have only met once. Yet, a private phone call he made to Gordie Howe's wife, Colleen, makes me wonder.

Mrs. Howe told my Mom that Marcel Aubut had phoned "out of the blue." In the conversation, he said that people were comparing her to Bonnie Lindros. Marcel then quickly added that he told people that there was "no comparison." Mrs. Howe retorted, "I'm sorry to hear that, Marcel!" I guess Mrs. Howe doesn't mind being compared to my Mom! We all laughed when we heard this story.

In the first game in the round-robin we got off to a slow start, tieing Finland 2–2. Their goaltender had stood on his head, but we didn't really play to our capabilities. Mike Keenan wanted to put a quick stop to that. He called a team meeting and wasted little time in getting down to business. Keenan talked with a lot of the veteran players about what we had to do and why we were all there. He'd say, "So-and-so, you've got a wife and a couple of kids. Wouldn't you rather be at the cottage?" "You, you've got a girlfriend. She's up at someplace. Wouldn't you rather be out there golfing?" He knew all the players were right where they wanted to be.

"We're here for a reason," said Keenan. "We've gone through all this preparation. Why waste it now?"

It was the truth. We'd worked too hard to throw it all away, and we quickly turned things around. We really started to click together as a unit and we easily won our next three games—6-3 over the U.S., 4-1 over Sweden and 6-2 against Czechoslovakia.

Keenan has an unbelievable will to win. He'd have us riding the bike after tough games, even if we were dead tired. He just wanted to make sure we stayed in shape. Still, you'd be thinking, "God, I'm exhausted!"

Steve Larmer was used to the way Keenan coached because he played for him on the Blackhawks, and he really helped me get used to his style. Sometimes you want to read a coach—try to guess what he's thinking, what he's going to ask you to do.

If I had any problems, Keenan would be the first one to help me out. I mean, there I was, eighteen years old, and I'd be sitting at the back of the plane playing cards with the big boys. He'd come back and make sure I wasn't getting in over my head. When we got on the plane, I usually hopped to the back because that's where the scoops were. You'd get to hear all the gossip that's going around the league.

Keenan was a stickler for details. I remember one day in practice I came out on the ice with the wrong color tape on my socks. I had red socks on and I was supposed to wear red tape. But I was in a rush to get on the ice and I had white tape on. I figured it was no big deal. Keenan blew a gasket on me.

"For crissakes, get him some red tape!"

Whoops! There I was, not wanting to upset anyone because I was one of the rookies on the team, and I've got the head coach steamed because I've managed to put the wrong tape on my socks. Believe me, I made sure I got some red tape—and fast.

The trainers were great. Juergen Merz bailed me out a number of times. I'd always go to the washroom between periods, but Keenan usually talked right up until the time we had to go back out on the ice. Then I had to run to the washroom, come right back, throw my gear on and go out. I was always the last guy out. Keenan said to Juergen one day in Montreal, "Don't let him be late. You're in charge of him."

"Okay, Mike, I take care of the kid," said Juergen.

I had a number of superstitions I had to follow between periods during the Canada Cup. One was having to go to the washroom, but I also taped my stick, tightened my skates—left before right—my gloves were always on the bench, not on the floor, and my helmet was usually on top of my gloves or beside them. It all depended on what was working at the time.

Although I was playing at a higher level than I ever had before, it was almost easier because I was playing with such great players. Everyone does his job, so, you've just got to do yours. My level of play picked up. The coaches got more confidence in me. My ice time improved. I had fun. That's what it's all about.

What they wanted me to do out there was establish a physical presence. It was my job to go out and hit. When the team was having a tough time, if I could go out and make a big hit to take somebody out, it might lift some of the other guys.

There was talk on the ice—they could hear me coming during the Canada Cup. Some guys would say, "Don't come near me, kid. I'm not in the mood."

Mike Keenan

Eric impressed the coaches right from the start. At one point during the first session the other four coaches came into the dressing room, and we all sat down and looked at each other. We were all thinking the same thing, but nobody said it. And then finally, I don't know exactly who it was, but one of us said, "This kid is a player." We all acknowledged right there that he was a special athlete. He was respectful and worked really hard. He was producing on the ice and competing on a daily basis and playing better than most of the fifty-odd players that we had in training camp.

One of the things I can recall vividly was his reaction after a pre-tournament game in Ottawa where he'd been the number one star. We walked through one of the back exits together with a couple of other players, and when Eric came out he busted loose across the football field at Lansdowne Park as if he was going for a touchdown pass. He'd been by far the best player in the game, and I think he started to realize he had a really good shot at making the team. It was eleven o'clock at night, it was raining, but he had to let loose a little bit. The bus was parked at the far end of the stadium field, so he just broke into a gallop. None of us really said much, but we all kind of giggled. We knew then that he had a good shot at making it as well.

One of his best nights might have been in an exhibition game at the Montreal Forum, where he turned the jeers to cheers. He played great. He played with emotion and passion. He played a physical game and he made a difference on the ice. He was one of the best players on the ice and was named first star—that's quite a statement. His ability to see the game and to see the ice was impressive considering the pressures that were on him. Many fans were on his back at the start because of the Nordiques situation, but by the end of the night everybody was supporting him because he just went out and competed. He didn't let anything distract him. He played the best hockey he could play and let that do the talking for him.

Eric was a physical force in the tournament. The check that knocked Samuelsson out of the tournament was an outstanding bodycheck, and it was completely legal. Samuelsson is a big, strong man. We also had Eric play against Joel Otto quite a bit when we faced the Americans, and he was really able to handle Otto—all 6' 5" of him. It was pretty impressive for a kid his age. Physically, we knew that Eric would be capable of doing it because he's got the physique. We just wanted to make sure he was mentally tough enough to deal with it. And he certainly was that.

At the same time, Eric was also a skilled enough hockey player to play on specialty teams. He played on the power play, he killed penalties, he logged a lot of ice time. He was one of the top players for us.

I think Eric is misunderstood. In my opinion, he's a really fine young man. He's taken a lot of harsh criticism that's not deserved, and I think he's handled himself extremely well for an individual who's been put through the pressures, the media pressures, the outside pressures, that he's had to go through. I've learned that people become jealous very quickly of others who are successful or have ability.

I was hounded by the media about my situation with the Quebec Nordiques throughout the tournament, but things really heated up as we were heading to Quebec City to play the Soviets in the final round-robin game. I was a little scared before the game. I mean, it's just a hockey game, but the media were reporting it like it was going to be a war. There were clips on Quebec television showing teenagers burning my sweaters in malls, jumping on them. And here I was, an eighteen-year-old kid trying to play hockey.

The media were grabbing at everything. Sometimes I handled it well and sometimes I didn't.

There was a lot of talk about me being anti-French. That's bull. I think it's great that the people of Quebec have a different heritage. Diversity is great. It would be pretty boring if we were all the same. I think it's great that Quebec is part of Canada.

I just don't feel the Nordiques care about winning. I can't be part of an organization where I don't sense that fierce commitment to be the best.

I've said publicly a number of times that I'd be very happy to play in Montreal—which is something those who accuse me of being anti-Quebec totally ignore. I think Pat Burns would be a great coach to play for. The Canadiens' organization has the will to win.

I read a speech by Ken Dryden about the Canadiens and how they've operated over the years. It was an incredible contrast to the way I feel the Nordiques run things. Dryden said: "In Montreal, it never seemed to matter much just who owned the team. What did matter was who wore the sweaters and who scored the goals. That's why people paid their money and went to games, and the Canadiens' owners never forget that. They may have enjoyed getting their names in the papers, being central to the main topic of conversation around the city, but they never pretended to be more important to the success of the team than they were or ever could be. They let public attention focus on, they gave responsibility to, those who could and had to deliver."

Dryden went on to say there was never any mistaking the team's ultimate purpose. "In all the time I played in Montreal, I never once had the feeling nor I'm sure did any of the other players, the fans, or the media nor the management or coaches that there was any other goal for the Montreal Canadiens than to win the Stanley Cup. Never once were we compromised; never once did we fear we would be. The owners never jumped in from the sidelines to fire their coaches or managers, just to remind everyone

who was in charge, whose team this really was, like George Stein-
brenner did. They never sold their Gretzkys and Messiers and
Fuhrs and Kurris like Peter Pocklington did, stripping assets out
of the team, out from under their players and fans, putting the
money into their own pockets and making the team poorer. . . .
With the Molsons and Bronfmans, in every action, in every deed,
their goal was our goal. To win the Stanley Cup. To be the best."

I just don't sense any of that same burning desire to win in the
Nordiques' organization. Marcel Aubut cheated the fans and his
players last year. The team missed the playoffs again for the fifth
straight year—not an easy feat when 16 out of 22 teams make the
playoffs each year. It's not likely they would have missed the
playoffs if they had traded me. Aubut knew there was no way I
was ever going to play for him. I have told him so. I have also met
privately with Pagé, his general manager, and separately with his
coach at the start of last season, Dave Chambers. There should
have been no doubt about my feelings. Even the Nordiques' best
player, Joe Sakic, came out and said they should have traded me,
and he took heat for that.

The stress on my family has been incredible. My Dad has a
full-time job, and yet every day and night he's dealing with my
situation. And my mother is forever being targetted. A Quebec
radio station held a contest awarding a prize to the person who
came up with the best Bonnie Lindros joke. Two different newspapers, including one in Quebec, published psychological pro-
files of our family as if we were criminals—done by psychiatrists
we'd never even met! Another Quebec publication had an edito-
rial cartoon portraying me wearing a Ku Klux Klan robe. And I'm
supposed to be the racist one? It was just too much.

They describe my mother as the person at the helm. Yet if you
look at the newspapers, there's not one quote from her to back
that up. There was a time I was really mad at my mother. I was
reading the press so much that I was becoming brainwashed by

people I now realize I can't trust. I was really upset. My Dad sat down with me and my Mom, and we had it out. I realized that a lot of people wanted to see our family divided, and I was falling right into the trap.

Then I got mad that they were picking on my Mom, when my Dad had said far more controversial things in the press. But because my Dad's a man, his comments are reported accurately.

All I can say is they must have a lot of fabricated information because, in fact, my Mom can only remember being interviewed by one French reporter, Bertrand Raymond, in September 1991.

Then the press came out with all these outlandish salary figures I was supposed to have asked for from Quebec. I don't want a penny from the Nordiques and I've never asked for one.

There's been so much pressure, but we always hung together. Whenever someone got down, there'd be someone around to boost their spirits. I would get down, and my Mom would be there for me. My Dad would get down, and I would be there for him. We all just helped each other out. My brother has started playing really good hockey, and that brought everyone up. My sister started settling into her new school, so that made my parents happy. This whole business has taken its toll, but we Lindroses are a pretty resilient bunch.

The Nordiques must have thought I would cave in. They were still talking about getting me to sign a contract after the Winter Olympics. I think there was a strategy to make it look like it was the people of Quebec I was rejecting, when in fact it was the Nordiques' management.

They held a big news conference for me the day before the Canada Cup game in Quebec City because of all the interview requests. Even when I wasn't in the dressing room there would be ten cameras there filming an empty stall. Sean Burke would come out of the showers and say, "Well, here I am, boys. One at a time. One at a time."

The team made sure I was as well prepared off the ice as I was on it. Bill Tuele, one of the team's public relations directors, who normally works for the Edmonton Oilers, really helped me out before the news conference. He briefed me. Keenan also came in to brief me. And then Pat Burns came in to brief me. They all cared. That felt good.

The news conference was really hostile. The Quebec media were firing darts at me. They were trying to turn my decision into an entirely political issue. I wasn't turning my back on a province, I was turning my back on a team. But I couldn't say it at the time as our objective was not to embarrass the Nordiques. The media, on the other hand, just wanted to sell newspapers, and I guess I was their ticket.

I think the guys on the team really felt sorry for me at times. None of the players said anything about my decision. They all knew the situation and understood it, including the French-speaking players. I never heard a negative thing about my decision, not one.

Other people would come up to me and say, "Why don't you try Quebec for a year or two, and then you can move on if you don't like it?" Well, for one thing, the Nordiques never offered me that option. Not once. In their first offer to me, just prior to the October deadline for signing juniors, they tried to tie me up with a ten-year deal.

What a lot of people don't realize is that there's no such thing as real free agency in the NHL. That was really drilled home to me again at the start of the Canada Cup when an NHL arbitrator awarded Scott Stevens to the New Jersey Devils after Brendan Shanahan signed as a free agent with St. Louis.

Stevens had just signed with St. Louis as a free agent the year before, and now all of a sudden he's got to pack up his family and move again. Some free agency! I was there when it happened. I felt bad for Brendan. I felt bad for Scott. You feel sorry for his wife and kids. He had just bought a new house in St. Louis. Scott Stevens is such a classy individual that he never made Shanny feel bad about it. I was walking down the hallway at Maple Leaf Gardens just after it happened and I saw Scott talking to his wife, his kids and his parents, from Kitchener, Ontario. You could just see the pain in their faces. Their whole lives had been uprooted.

Shanny went to St. Louis because he felt they would have a winner soon. He didn't think the arbitration would cost the club a great player like Scott Stevens. Not that Brendan's not a great player, but he's a forward and Scott's a defenseman. There's a greater demand for defensemen with Scott Stevens's talent, aggressiveness, size and strength. That just reinforced in my mind that I'd better not go near the Nordiques.

Even now, the organization is claiming there have been no trade offers for me, and it is quick to threaten any team who calls its management with tampering charges. The Nordiques are assuming that teams coming forth with offers must have met directly with me or my family prior to making the offer. That's what it would be like if I signed with Quebec—Aubut could say that no offer was good enough to trade me away. He'd drag me through my whole hockey career in a city where the team's goal is not to win hockey games. I'm a person who loves sports and who loves to win. And not to have that opportunity would make everything futile.

OTHER VOICES:

Brendan Shanahan

When we were in Quebec City for the game with the Soviets, we made sure Eric was never alone. We didn't want anybody to come up to him and try something—you never know what to expect.

I think the whole situation was a bit too much. Eric would lead you to believe that it didn't bother him at all, that he was totally insensitive to it. But the truth is, I think it really did get to him.

I've agreed with him on the issue with the Nordiques right from the start. Even before I knew Eric, I agreed. It wasn't like he could go and play in Quebec for a couple years and then become a free agent.

The way I see it, there's got to be a happy medium. We can't have all the players choosing to play for the New York Rangers or the Los Angeles Kings. But at the same time, you have to respect the fact that Eric has earned some say in his future. He has made Eric Lindros the best player in the world for his age, and he should have some control over where he spends the next fifteen years of his life. Is the elite doctor, the elite lawyer, dictated to about what city and what country they have to live in? If Eric's conviction is so strong that he's willing to sit out an entire year, or two years, then, whether you think he's right or wrong, you have to respect the guy for sticking to his convictions.

The thing that impressed me most about Eric as a player was that he seemed like a guy who wanted to continue to learn new things and improve himself. We skated together a few times before the Canada Cup training camp started. He was the first guy after a hard day's skating, when a lot of other guys were going off the ice, to come up to me and say, "Hey, Shanny, let's do a little passing drill, let's go shoot on the goalie."

I remember one day he was curious as to how he would do against NHL players in a fight. So after practice we dropped our gloves and grabbed onto each other to throw some mock punches. He grabbed me and kind of gave me the "scarecrow"— that's when a guy grabs you and starts shaking you. It looks like you don't have a bone in your body; you're just being swung around like a scarecrow. He gave me a couple of Barney Rubble bumps on the head, too. He was so strong, and he was throwing some wild punches—I think one of them accidentally hit me in the side of the head. Tie Domi, one of the NHL's heavyweight contenders, was there, too. He was instructing both of us, and he said, "Don't worry, Eric. I think you'll be okay."

Eric could turn around the entire tempo of a game without even touching the puck. I remember against Sweden, Keenan sat him out one shift. It was in the middle of the game; there was a bit of a lull. When he opened the door to let Eric out, Eric was so fired up, he just went out and crushed a few guys with hits. It was awesome. On that same shift, he put Ulf Samuelsson out. And those were big, clean, hard hits, not cheap shots. It's like, "Here I am. I'm coming. My elbows are down and I'm going to run you over." It was a head-on challenge—and Eric won them all. Once Eric would start hitting, it would start a chain reaction. Corson would go run a guy over. Rick Tocchet would go run a guy over. It would make you want to run somebody over.

One thing Eric could not do, though, was carry a tune. Whenever he'd get into my car, he'd go rifling through my CDs. He wanted to listen to REM's "Shiny Happy People." He would sing his heart out to that song. And I discovered I wasn't the worst singer in the world—there is somebody worse than me. He's an awful singer!

The whole Canada Cup experience must have been quite an adjustment for him. He went from a world of sixteen-, seventeen-year-old guys in junior hockey to hanging out with men. Men who are talking about buying property and mortgages and insurance policies. It must have been a big difference from talking about high school parties and fake I.D. But he never looked like he was out of place.

It was a team where guys really looked out for one another. I know that was certainly the case with Eric when we were in Quebec City. We all wanted to deflect that pressure that was on him. We all kind of felt bad, and we just wanted him to go out and have a great game. You wanted him to succeed. We tried to shelter him from it as much as we could, to just be around him and keep him happy and distract him. That was a lot of pressure for an eighteen-year-old guy. It had gone beyond a sports issue and become a national, cultural issue. Why?

Despite all the tension, I wound up having a really good time in Quebec City. I had a great afternoon the day before the game eating at one of those outdoor patio places. I was sitting there with Corson and Shanahan and some of our coaches—Pat Burns, Tom Webster and Brian Sutter. We had a lot of laughs, and Burns kept on getting one of the local musicians to play some of his old favorites. Shanny was singing. It was pretty brutal!

I didn't find it uncomfortable in the city. When people recognized me, they would usually sit there and stare and point. I don't think they hated me.

The game against the Soviets never lived up to its build-up. What could live up to that kind of hype? On CTV Sports, in their preview to the game, they described me as "Public Enemy Number 1" in Quebec City. They wanted conflict; they wanted to go for the hard sell. But they didn't get what they were looking for. It was really anticlimactic.

I was nervous at the start. My skates were going a hundred miles an hour—my feet were moving, but I wasn't doing anything. I think I was trying too hard to prove something. The effort was there, but it wasn't happening. Then something finally clicked for me. Paul Coffey made a good pass out in front and the puck went off a skate and over to me. I was sort of hanging around the back door and I chipped it in past the Soviet goal-tender to tie the score at 1-1. The fans at the Coliseum gave me a pretty good cheer. Some fans even gave me a standing ovation. Patty Burns came down to the end of the bench and gave me a pat and sort of looked at me funny. "Way to go, kid."

For the most part, I felt the fans were behind me that day. The fans in Quebec City love their hockey. They're dying to have a winning team in that city. Some spectators were holding up signs welcoming me to Quebec City, but the newspaper *Le Soleil* later reported that that had been orchestrated by the Nordiques, who had apparently supplied the fans with free tickets.

Actually, I had it a lot easier on the ice than my parents did in the stands. Carl and Bonnie decided to make the trip as a show of support. They were also there that day to meet with Aubut, but he wasn't at the meeting because the final deadline for signing the arena lease was expiring—that evening—and Marcel still had some negotiating left to do!

My parents had a French bodyguard on the advice of a reporter from a Montreal newspaper and were in a private box, but some fans recognized them early in the third period. The fans became unruly; they started to poke signs and sticks into the box, and they tried to climb through. My Dad said it was the first time he'd ever seen my Mom scared. When the security guard went to check about ushering them through the back door, he saw that the hallway was completely filled with more fans. They had to get police to clear the hallway so they could exit through the back door to a waiting car.

They didn't get to stay for the end of the game, but then they didn't miss much. It was a real yawner. The game wound up in a 3-3 tie. It certainly wasn't a classic Canada-Soviet matchup. In fact, the Soviets had one of their weaker teams and failed to make the playoffs in the Canada Cup.

With the Quebec City game out of the way, we could finally

concentrate on the business at hand—winning another Canada Cup title for our country.

I think the thing that made our team stand out above the others was heart. We wanted it so badly. I don't think we necessarily had the most skilled team, but we had more heart than any other team. I think Sweden had the most skilled team, but I don't think they wanted it as much. When we defeated them in the semifinals, there was just no doubt that we were the hungrier team.

The Canada Cup finals were an all-North American affair for the first time, as the United States defeated Finland in the other semifinal to advance. The Americans had a great team. They had good speed up front and a super defense corps. They had a lot of guys playing really well. Jeremy Roenick was scared to death he was going to be traded from Chicago to the Nordiques in a deal for me, so he had a great tournament. We were yapping at each other about that. I'd tell him, "Have fun in Quebec." And he'd say, "Have fun back in junior, because I'm not going." Roenick comes to play and he works hard. Steve Larmer really respects him—and if Steve Larmer respects him, he deserves respect.

While we were wary of the Americans, we still felt we had the better team. It was a best-of-three final, but we were determined not to let it go the distance. We came out strong in the first game in Montreal to win 4-1, but we lost Wayne Gretzky in that game. He wound up with a back injury that sidelined him for the rest of the tournament.

It was amazing to see the way Mark Messier took over after Gretzky went down. He just got that look. With Messier, it's in the eyes. They're like lasers. Man, do they ever get you going. I was sitting on the other side of the room to the right when Messier stood up to make a speech and said what needed to be said.

We wanted to make sure we wrapped it up heading into game two in Hamilton, because anything could happen if it came down to a third and deciding game. We had the killer instinct. As Messier said, "Let's get 'er done!"

The game was really tight through two periods and was tied 2-2 in the third. Then Steve Larmer took over. It all happened in a flash. As soon as Larmer stole the puck from Gary Suter at our blue line, we knew the puck was going in. The whole bench stood up. We were thinking, "Larms has got the puck. We know we've won." He just raced in on a breakaway and put it between Mike Richter's legs. If there was one guy who deserved to score that winning goal, it was Larms.

I was sitting at the far end of the bench in the final moments of the game. As one of the young guys on the team, I knew I wasn't going to see any action. As a matter of fact, I didn't see anything—I was praying with my head bowed between my legs. Luc Robitaille was right beside me doing the same thing. One of our coaches, Brian Sutter, came up behind me and said, "Lad, get yer head up." I didn't move. He hit me. "Lad, get yer head up." I turned around and yelled, "I'm praying!" and put my head back down. Sutter started laughing. Corson was howling. And Keenan and Burns were laughing, too.

Dirk Graham finally scored into the empty net to clinch it. "Duke" was a latecomer, and Keenan took a lot of grief for having him on the team because he was from Keenan's team, the Blackhawks. But he was a big contributor. He was a great defensive player. He got the job done at both ends.

Finally, the buzzer sounded. The crowd at Copps Coliseum was a sea of Canadian flags. The national anthem was played. We all got to hold the Canada Cup trophy and get our picture taken with it. It was a great feeling carrying it. I don't know if it gets any better. We were like a family. Guys like Al MacInnis and Paul Coffey, who go head-to-head against each other all year in competition in the NHL, were hugging and enjoying the moment. That's what it's all about.

I sat there with Shanahan and Corson in the dressing room afterwards. Our attitude was, "It's over. We did it. We came. We conquered. Let's enjoy it." So we started whistling. It was an unbelievable feeling to win, but you also were hit with the realization that this team would never be again. The next time around, some will have retired, others will have moved into different roles, new faces will be coming in.

I think what I will remember more than anything are the friendships. I just learned so much from all of the guys. They were such class acts, on and off the ice. If I was a bigger sponge, I'd be a better person. There was so much information available to be learned that I wish I could have absorbed even more.

The day after the tournament ended, I went into the Leafs dressing room to pick up my equipment. Paul Coffey was there with a friend's golden retriever. We sat around and shot the breeze for a while. Paul was a great guy to play with. He's a quiet guy, really his own person. When the American coach Bob Johnson became ill with a brain tumor at the start of the tournament, Paul was really down. He loved playing for Johnson, who was his coach with the Pittsburgh Penguins. I found I could relate to Paul, because he's not the kind of guy to let anyone push him around. He looked out for me, he helped me out, and I felt comfortable being around him.

By this time, the Leafs had opened their training camp, and my old Oshawa teammate Robbie Pearson was on the ice, taking his shot at making it in the NHL. Dave Hannan, who was then with the Leafs, walked into the dressing room and made a crack when he saw me. "Oh God, the rumor's true!" There were rumors flying around at the time that I was going to get traded by the Nordiques to the Maple Leafs. It hurt seeing Robbie Pearson on the ice at practice. I was happy for him, but I wanted to be there too.

It felt good that we had won the Canada Cup. I was thankful to have had a chance to prove myself. I tried to do my best with it.

It was like getting my foot in the door. But now that foot was really about to get squeezed.

The big question all the Team Canada players were asking each other was, "How much time are you getting off before training camp?" Some guys had two days, others had three days, some had four days before they had to report to their NHL training camps. Me, I was looking at possibly two years.

12

Behind Closed Doors

Rick Curran

Sometimes, when I look back at the events of the last few years, I have to wonder just how determined the Nordiques were to have Eric on their team. Just how far were the Nordiques willing to go to ensure that they would be holding Eric's ticket in the 1991 NHL Entry Draft Sweepstakes?

I remember a conversation I had with Dave Chambers while he was head coach of the Nordiques. It was in the hallway of the Meadowlands Arena in New Jersey, on January 24, about halfway through the 1990-91 season. The Nordiques had just lost again, this time 6–1 to the Devils, but they still weren't far from fourth place and the final playoff position. I couldn't believe they had started Scott Gordon in goal for what was obviously a crucial game for both teams. But when I asked what was going on, Chambers said that the coaching staff had been given instructions to go with the players they had and not to worry too much about the win–loss record.

Just what was going on? When you take a look at events, it really makes you stop and think. Consider, for example, these two rather interesting player transactions that season:

• November 17, 1990: The Nordiques traded veterans Aaron Broten, Lucien DeBlois and Michel Petit to the desperate Toronto Maple Leafs for rookie Scott Pearson and two second-round draft picks. Pearson scored a goal in his first game with the Nordiques—and was then sent to the minors following that same game.

• January 17, 1991: The Nordiques traded veteran defenseman Joe Cirella (currently with the New York Rangers, who finished in first place in the 1991-92 regular season) for college player Aaron Miller and a fifth-round draft pick. Neither of the acquired players played regularly in the 1991-92 season.

Why would a team struggling to make the playoffs trade away four contributing veterans and have nothing in the lineup to show for it? Why would an organization looking to win use an incredible total of 52 players over the course of just one season with the net result of coming in dead last?

Perhaps this might explain why Marcel Aubut simply refused to accept our suggestion of a pre-draft trade. During our meetings in Quebec City last July, Marcel suggested that it was only fair for Eric to sign with the Nordiques because they had earned the right to him by finishing last. Carl replied that Eric didn't think it was so fair—because the Nordiques appeared to have *chosen* to finish

ast. I vividly recall Marcel's abrupt response: "I don't want to
alk about that!"

Professional basketball wisely recognized the need to protect
eams from themselves. It introduced a lottery system among non-
playoff teams to ensure that an orchestrated last-place finish
loesn't necessarily reward the culprit with first choice in the draft.

Once we'd resigned ourselves to the fact that Eric was going
o be drafted by the Nordiques, we wanted to arrange to meet
with Marcel Aubut immediately after the draft. However, Marcel
had an asking price for the timely meeting: Eric had to agree to
out the Nordiques' sweater on at the draft podium. Eric had
already given it a lot of thought, and he had decided that it would
be inappropriate for him to make such a misleading public ges-
ure. As a result, the Nordiques delayed our first meeting until
he end of July, a wait of over five weeks.

Our "confidential" meeting finally took place in Quebec City
n a presidential suite of the beautiful Chateau Frontenac Hotel.
The meeting began on July 31 and went through to the next
morning. Carl and I met with Marcel, his general manager Pierre
Pagé and a partner from the team's public accounting firm. We
presented the reasons why we didn't think the Nordiques and
Eric were a good fit; the club spent their time explaining why Eric
hould plan on playing out his career in a Nordiques' uniform.

At no time during the meeting did we come forward with any
ontract proposal, despite what was later reported by the Quebec
media. It should have been quite clear to anyone in that room that
we were there to negotiate a trade not a contract. We politely
nformed the Nordiques that it just wasn't meant to be, and they
advised us that they had no intention of making a trade.

Our concern has always been this: Once Eric was there, would
he ever be able to get out? Or would signing that first contract
essentially mean a long-term commitment to the Nordiques,
egardless of the years specified in the first contract?

The big news in hockey at that time concerned Brendan Shanahan. He had just completed his first NHL contract with New Jersey and was now categorized as a "Type 1" free agent, meaning that he was free to negotiate with the team of his choice. He had signed with the St. Louis Blues. However, St. Louis and New Jersey could not agree on what the Blues had to give the Devils as compensation (players, money, draft picks or a combination thereof). Consequently, the NHL rules called for an arbitrator appointed by the league to rule on the compensation.

The concern at the time was that the arbitrator could decide to overcompensate the player's former team, either in error or with the intent of discouraging future free agency transactions. And that's what seemed to have happened when the decision came in a few weeks later. St. Louis ended up losing Scott Stevens, one of the premier defensemen in the league. The Blues had paid a high price for signing Stevens as a free agent the previous year: it had cost them five first-round draft picks. After witnessing that result, any team was going to be wary of signing that type of free agent and possibly having to deal with the arbitrator.

It's a particular worry for a premium hockey player, a franchise player. In a trade involving those players, an arbitrator has extreme difficulty in assessing what would be fair compensation. Wayne Gretzky, for example, has said that there might not be any fair compensation if Eric continues to evolve as a player in the way he has. We were facing an extremely complicated situation, one in which we just didn't feel safe.

After our lengthy breakfast meeting with Aubut and Pagé, Carl and I talked things over at the airport, waiting for our flight to Dorval. Could we really expect a club to come forward in a couple of years and sign Eric, knowing that they might be risking the loss of the entire nucleus of their team? At the very least, the team could lose so many key players that signing Eric would mean running the risk of weakening the club, not strengthening it. Was there a way to break the apparent logjam with the Nordiques before things got messy?

One thought led to another, and we began to try to figure out whether there might not be a way to ensure a trade without the threat of arbitration. We came up with the idea of a pre-established formula for fair compensation in a trade, so that the NHL's arbitration process would not be needed. In the event that Eric requested a trade to another club following two years' play, the Nordiques would have a limited time to make a suitable deal. If they appeared to be taking an unreasonable amount of time to complete the transaction, then we would be allowed to seek our own trade, using the following pre-established formula, defining: 1) the number of players, 2) how they would be picked and 3) the number of draft picks, as fair compensation for the Nordiques.

I suggested the idea to Marcel the next day. He quickly said it would be unacceptable. Although the reason he gave was that such a deal would be against NHL bylaws, his response was so quick and decisive I doubted the Nordiques would ever be willing to discuss a short-term deal of any kind.

OTHER VOICES:

Gordon Kirke (Eric's lawyer)

Eric is a strong-willed individual, but he's also a member of a very strong and close family unit. They work together on important decisions in any of the children's lives. It's a very warm and loving family, and it's gratifying to be included as an adviser. It's

been a very trying time for them; Bonnie, in particular, has taken
a lot of flak. But I can tell you, she certainly has Eric's best interests at heart.

At first, I thought the family's position with regard to the
Nordiques was simply a matter of personal preference. I quickly
realized, though, that there were substantial logical reasons for it.

One thing that has to be made clear is that Eric is not challenging the NHL draft. He is not bucking the system. The rules say
that a junior player who is drafted can sit out the two years—it's
up to the team drafting him to try to sign him or trade him. Eric's
not bucking the system; he's playing strictly in accordance with
the NHL rules.

On the other hand, look at what's going on in the NHL Entry
Draft. When Vancouver and Buffalo came into the league, they
were given first and second draft picks in the year of their drafting. And I understand that, this coming year, Ottawa and Tampa
Bay will be given first and second picks. It's traditional in sports.
If you look at all the sports leagues, the expansion teams get first
or second pick, depending on how many expansion teams are
coming in.

But what happens the year Eric Lindros is eligible for the
draft? Here's this unusual—almost mystical—arrangement that
results in the Nordiques getting a number-one draft pick, in the
first round only, ahead of the expansion team in San Jose. That's
baffling to me.

I don't think the Nordiques are under any illusion about Eric
playing for them. It's absolutely clear. Eric is a very competitive
individual and he wants to play for a team he believes has a winning attitude and the desire to win. He doesn't believe that's the
case in Quebec, and I think that's eminently clear. I don't know
what more anyone could do to convince them of the truth of this
statement.

Eric is certainly not anti-Quebec City. He has nothing against the people of Quebec. It's the team, the organization. He chooses not to play for the Nordiques.

Challenging the NHL draft in court is certainly an option, although it's not something we're pursuing at the moment. In the course I teach at the law schools, we've reviewed this sort of situation over the last seven years, quite apart from Eric. And I think if you look at the situation, the NHL draft is probably the most oppressive and restrictive draft system in pro sports. You look at the period of time the drafting team has to sign its new talent—there's no effective free agency. Then you consider how Quebec was able to get the first pick, ahead of the expansion team, which I think is unusual in sports. You add to that the Nordiques' conduct since the draft, and I don't think you have to be a legal scholar to think that anybody challenging the NHL draft would have a pretty fair shot at it.

We never wanted to infuriate Marcel, as that might lead him to punish Eric rather than trade his rights for the good of the Nordiques. However, last January I met Marcel in the Montreal airport just before the Winter Olympics. When it became clear to him that I wasn't there to discuss a contract, he lost it. In Marcel's words: "There is no f——— way an eighteen-year-old is going to tell me what to do! We are taking off the gloves!"

OTHER VOICES:

Carl Lindros

People have often asked us whether we've wavered in all of this—whether we've wondered if we were really doing the right thing. Well, if anything, the months since the NHL draft have only strengthened our belief that we were doing what was right.

We couldn't risk a long-term relationship when the fit was so bad. One of our biggest concerns has always been the track record of the Quebec Nordiques. The events of the past season have only magnified our concerns.

I wasn't surprised that on August 2, Marcel Aubut abruptly rejected our concept of a two-year deal. I spoke with the Nordiques' assistant general manager, Gilles Léger, on March 2 of this year and he told me, "We were stubborn not to have seriously considered your proposal."

We were very disturbed to hear Nordiques general manager Pierre Pagé say publicly that Eric should be fair and give Quebec a try. "Maybe a year later, or two years later, we could trade him if he wants, if he doesn't like it. But at least be fair and give Quebec a shot," was the way Pagé put it, months after the club had rejected that very proposal.

After Marcel Aubut offered us a ten-year, $50-million deal in September, 1991—an offer he would later, on national television, deny having made—I told him that even if he offered a one-year contract that somehow included an iron-clad trade, I didn't think it would ever work after all that had happened. It would be like sleeping on dynamite. The fans, the players and the coaches would all know that Eric was just passing through for a year. At this point, the only thing to do is just move forward.

People in Quebec City have referred to Marcel as the grand negotiator—a man full of tricks. We have suspicions that the conflict has been presented in the Quebec media as English versus French so as to enhance the likelihood of federal government grants for the new arena that Marcel Aubut argues is so badly needed. We were prepared to let Eric be portrayed as a mercenary, spoiled brat if that meant a trade would be done. However, to be portrayed as a racist was just too much. I also suspect that the attacks on Bonnie fit within a strategy of isolating Eric from his family.

I've heard that Marcel Aubut has had a mission to get Eric in a Nordiques' sweater since Eric was sixteen years old, and that Marcel considers this his biggest personal challenge. Whether or not Marcel is on a one-man crusade to sign Eric, the fact is that this just isn't a good fit, for reasons that are beyond Marcel's control and because of other factors that are too late to change. Eric has endured more than enough, as has our whole family. There has no doubt also been strain on the Nordiques: on their players, their coaching staff, their fans—and, I suspect, even on Marcel.

To me, the biggest challenge for Marcel should be to effectively trade Eric and to prove in the seasons ahead that, contrary to all appearances, he does care about winning. Not for himself, but for his fans and for his players.

Digging for Gold

It was a long skate back to the bench—probably my longest ever. The first shoot-out in Olympic hockey history had just begun. We were playing against the Germans in the quarterfinals. If we lost this game, we could kiss our medal hopes good-bye. I was the first shooter for Team Canada . . . and I'd just missed.

It was a sick feeling. Not only do you feel that you've let your team down, but you've let your country down. The TV cameras are all focused on your face. You can feel it. As you get to the bench, it's as if you've got a skin disease. All the players move away. No one's around you because they don't know what to say. What are they going to say? "Nice try"?

I was mad at myself for missing. You *can't* miss those. I was sitting there, thinking, "If we lose, that's it, I'm toast . . . over one shoot-out, over one breakaway."

We had finished first in our pool after the round-robin portion of the tournament, and no one expected the Germans to give us much trouble. But the score was tied 3-3 after sixty minutes of regulation time and another ten minutes of overtime. Now it was down to the shoot-out—five of our shooters against five of theirs in what amounted to a penalty-shot contest. There was so much at stake with every shot. With Sean Burke in goal for us, though, there was a real sense of confidence on our team. Burkie had been great throughout the tournament. Still, we had to score the goals for him.

It had been a frustrating game. We had three goals called back by the referee. Also, the Germans played a system where they had one forechecker and four men back. I don't care who you're playing—I don't care if you're playing Team Egypt—they're going to be tough to go in and beat when they've got four men back all the time. They just dumped the puck out to center ice, and a couple of players made some nice moves and put the puck in the net when they had the chance. I don't know if their goalie, Helmut De Raaf, was good or just lucky, but he was always there. He robbed me right at the end of overtime. Joey Juneau had set me up with a nice pass right in front and my shot hit the goalie's skate blade.

It was pretty tense being the first player in the shoot-out. When I moved in, I had the goaltender going to the left a little bit, and his glove was way down. The top shelf was wide open. I took a chip shot. But I should have used a seven-iron instead of a nine-iron—the puck went just over the top corner. Dave Hannan, who'd joined the team from the Toronto Maple Leafs just before the Olympics, told me the puck was bouncing a bit on the ice just as I shot it. Whether he was right or wrong, his comment made me feel better. I didn't have my eye on the puck. All I knew was that I missed.

I was in a daze after that. I sat at the back of the bench. I was trying to concentrate on what was going on in the shoot-out but I was having a tough time.

Meanwhile, Burkie turned back the Germans' first shot . . .

Dave Archibald missed for us . . .

Burkie made another save on the Germans . . .

Jason Woolley buried one upstairs to put us ahead 1-0 . . .

Burkie made a great glove-save on the Germans . . .

Wally Schreiber scored on a deke to make it 2-0 . . .

The Germans scored to close it to 2-1 . . .

Joe Juneau missed for us . . .

The Germans scored on their final shot to tie it 2-2 . . .

Suddenly it was a sudden-death shoot-out! As soon as the German player scored to tie it, I jumped right out on the ice. We had another shot at winning, and I didn't want to waste it. I don't think any of us realized how close we were to elimination at that point. Most of the guys on the bench were thinking, "We've come too far for it to end like this." I couldn't have agreed more.

The Olympics came at the perfect time for me; I'd been having a difficult time adjusting back to junior hockey in Oshawa after playing in the Canada Cup. I remember one of our early games, in Detroit. I just couldn't motivate myself at all. I was skating around the ice thinking, "Don't touch me. I don't want to be here. Just leave me alone." That's not the way I play but I just didn't have focus. Guys I used to play against were getting the better of me because I just wasn't there.

My whole spirit started going downhill. My desire to win just went out the window. I didn't care. I had already proven myself at what some would call the highest level. I went from playing on a power play with Wayne Gretzky, Luc Robitaille, Paul Coffey and Al MacInnis to playing with players right out of midget hockey. I was frustrated to be back at square one, and I didn't deal with it very well.

It was the first time I'd ever lost the drive to succeed, and it really scared me. My work ethic in practice faltered at times in a way it never had before. I felt sorry for my teammates, and for the fans, because I was letting them down.

The drive was rekindled for a while, for about eight or nine junior games, but the light at the end of the tunnel was always getting a shot with the Olympic team. That's what I kept myself focused on.

The World Junior Championships in Fussen, Germany, in late December ended up being a disappointment. We finished sixth after having won the gold medal two years in a row. I didn't play all that well, but no one played superbly. I think illness was one of the factors. We all got the flu. I had it, and so did Trevor Kidd, who was on loan from the Olympic team to play in goal. I weighed 216 pounds, and I'm usually at 230 or 232. I tried my best, but, of course, I took most of the heat from the press for our poor performance.

It seemed like it took forever, but the Winter Olympics in Albertville, France, finally did roll around. There were so many changes in personnel on the team leading up to the Olympic Games that I don't think we really started coming together as a unit until our final training camp in Davos, Switzerland. The pace at practice really picked up then. It was time to get down to business.

We played in the Globen Cup tournament in Sweden just before the Olympics. Most of the top teams were there, and it was a good warm-up to the main event. I had a lot of fun there with Dave Hannan, who was playing his first games with us. The tournament organizers gave out a flask to the most valuable player for each team after every game. Hannan would come into the dressing room before each game and say, "Well, I'm goin' for the flask tonight." So we had this little joke competition going about who was going to get the flask. Neither of us ever won it. But we played our hearts out as a team and we won the tournament. Sean Burke made 47 saves to help us beat the Swedes, who were the gold-medal favorites.

The tournament really brought our team together. We knew we could do well if we just played our game. Players don't know how good they can be. It's not just wizard coaching, it's not just super systems, it's not just flowing talents—it's confidence that wins games. That's what it's all about. We found a way to tap into it in Sweden and we did just fine. We started playing well, things started clicking at practice, and suddenly we had confidence.

Heading into the Olympics, most people figured we would be doing great just to pull off a bronze medal—Canada hadn't won a medal of any kind in Olympic hockey in twenty-four years. But we weren't thinking in those terms. We wanted to go in and do the best job possible and take our best shot. Our attitude was: "We're going to write our own story. We'll get what we deserve."

It was tough seeing players get cut from the team just before the Olympics. One player I was really sorry to see let go was Chris Kontos, who was released a week before the Olympics after being with the team for several months. I had a pretty good friendship with him. We went out together all the time. We'd be out there before and after practice working on things together—one-timers and passes. It really hurt to see him get cut. But I guess that's sports—that's part of doing what you think you have to do in order to win.

We got fitted for our Olympic team clothing in Annecy, France. We really started to get into it at that point, to realize that this was going to be more than just another tournament. It was neat getting suited up. Canada had switched its colors from the traditional red and white to purple and white. I thought the new colors were pretty sharp. After that, we had the day off. Dave

Hannan and I went for haircuts, and they served champagne afterwards. It was the best haircut I've ever had!

I think there were a lot of guys at the Olympics who had something to prove. It was a unique combination of ex-NHLers, current NHLers, others who'd been playing in Europe and guys hoping for their first—or another—NHL shot. There were a lot of unsung heroes on the team—guys like Dave Tippett, Dave Hannan, Curt Giles, Fabian Joseph, Brian Tutt, Todd Brost. They each brought a special set of talents to the rink, and it all worked together to create a successful team chemistry.

Curt Giles is someone I really enjoyed being around. The team's pre-Olympic schedule could be a real grind at times, but he made things a lot easier to get through. He's always upbeat. He's a super person. When things got rough and there were four-teen-hour bus rides, I'd look over at him, and I'd think, "If he's doing it—after all, he's been in 'The Show' for twelve years as an NHLer—then I guess I should do it, too." He would always give me advice, and he tried to make sure I wasn't putting too much pressure on myself. He'd say, "Just play to the best of your abil-ity—same as we expect from everybody else."

Curt Giles

If you just stand back and look at Eric as this teenage hockey phenomenon who's supposed to be the next big star in the NHL, you'll never really get a chance to know him. It's not fair to him, and it's not fair to yourself.

It was really funny at first, because I was intimidated by him. I'd heard so much about him being a great player, so we'd get on the ice and I'd try to send him that perfect pass. One day I just slapped myself and said, "Hey, this guy is just a person! Just play and do whatever you usually do."

When Eric first joined the Olympic team and we went over to Europe, he played extremely well. In the first four games he had something like three game-winning goals and one game-tying goal. He just kept getting better and better. But the expectations from the media and the fans were incredible. Every place we went it was "The Eric Lindros Show." It was always "ERIC LINDROS . . . and the Canadian Olympic Team." When you're eighteen years old and the media put that kind of pressure on you, you eventually put that kind of pressure on yourself, too.

I saw Eric struggling with that and I tried to help him out. I talked to him, tried to tell him just to be himself. We didn't need him to be a superman. We didn't need him to dominate games. We didn't need him to carry the torch for us. All we needed was for Eric Lindros to come and play like Eric Lindros could.

When people put you in a certain position, when they tell you you have to do this and you have to do that, after a while you start believing it and you start saying, "I've got to do more. I've got to do more." And while you're trying to do more and trying to do more, you're actually doing less. The expectations of Eric Lindros were so high that I think he started to feel that he wasn't doing enough.

The good thing about the Olympic Games was that we were isolated from everybody else. Nobody could get to Eric, and Eric could be himself. Eric just has to act like Eric, and that's when he plays his best hockey.

I think he was really shaken up by what happened at the World Juniors. He was expected to make the difference between gold and silver, and they wound up winning nothing. The majority of the blame was put on Eric because he was expected to carry the team. I think it was a big mistake to make him captain when he hadn't spent that much time with the team—it was just more pressure.

The thing is, nobody expects Eric to get shaken up. Nobody expects Eric to get nervous. Nobody expects Eric to get tired. Nobody expects Eric to not play well. All they expect from Eric is great things. They expect him to dominate all the time. It's not humanly possible.

To tell you the truth, I wouldn't want to be in his shoes for anything. There's so much pressure on Eric it's unbelievable. The thing is, I couldn't care less how he succeeds in hockey. I couldn't care less if he quit hockey tomorrow. I just want to see Eric be happy with his life. No matter what Eric does, I hope he succeeds in it, and, more important than that, I hope he's happy.

Sean Burke was another person who really anchored the team. The Olympic team is based in Calgary, and I lived with Burkie while we were out there. I think he gave the Olympic team more than just excellent goaltending—he gave us great leadership. He's a very steady, stable guy, and he can settle players down when things aren't going well. He communicated really well with everybody—from the players to the coaching staff to the trainers.

Burkie's also an unbelievable competitor. When you look back over your shoulder before a face-off at center ice and you see this totally focused, big guy in goal, you get this great feeling of confidence.

Burkie's situation with the New Jersey Devils was another eye-opener concerning the status of a so-called free agent in the

NHL. He had played out his option with New Jersey because he wanted to go to a team where he would get a shot at being the starting goaltender—he had been the starter with the Devils but was then relegated to backup and seemed stuck there. He was classified a free agent because he had played out his option, but any team that might have wanted to sign him was scared off by the incredibly high compensation they would have to pay New Jersey under the NHL's free agency rules. As a result, the only way he could really switch teams was if New Jersey traded him.

New Jersey was stringing him along, so Burkie decided to join the Olympic team rather than consider re-signing with the Devils—despite the lost income. It was a matter of principle.

Joe Juneau is another classy individual. He really sees the ice and knows where to go. He's a smart hockey player. We read each other really well, and we worked well together on the power play. We had a lot of fun moving that puck around. I really enjoyed working with a player of his talents. The Boston Bruins are lucky to have him.

Joe Juneau

I think playing for three different teams during the year was really tough for Eric. I can remember one day when the Olympic team was playing in Montreal. I was his roommate. He arrived in town for the game after being with one of his other teams, and he came into the room without a suitcase. He'd come up with nothing but his hockey equipment and four hockey sticks. He had no extra clothes—just the suit he was wearing. Actually, he told me that he hadn't known where he was going that day until the last second. Someone had just told him, "You're playing tonight in Montreal." That's when I realized how hard it must be for him. It was a big game, and he got booed the whole time, but he still played well.

Personally, I don't think his decision not to sign with the Nordiques is because he doesn't like the people of Quebec. I'm French-Canadian, and I never had any trouble with Eric at all. At the Olympics, I got along with his Dad very well, too. I remember one night I spent an hour talking with his Dad about all sorts of things.

I had some good times with Eric, especially in France during the Olympics. We would send each other messages on the Olympic computer system. We would write about funny things that happened in the games or in practices, or make jokes about each other. We also had a lot fun sliding down the ski hills on the trays from the cafeteria.

It was Joey and I who came up with the idea of sledding in the Olympic Village a few days before the Games started. There was nothing to do at night, so we borrowed some of the cafeteria trays and decided to go tobogganing. It was Curt Giles who suggested using the trays, because it was something he'd done in college— we were just going to slide down on our jackets.

We were staying at a big ski resort, so the hills were perfectly groomed. You could really get rocking! We'd be out there for about three hours just having a riot. It was something that broke up the monotony and the tension. It was a chance to be a kid again. I must admit, though, at 6' 5" and 232 pounds, it's not easy getting your butt on a cafeteria tray!

The Olympic computer system was another source of amusement. I practically lived on it. I'd send messages to guys on our team, or to some of the other Canadian athletes. I even exchanged messages with the skiers up in Val d'Isere. When any Canadians won a medal, I sent a message congratulating them.

The different venues were too spread out, so it was hard to mingle with the other athletes in Albertville. It took away a bit from the atmosphere, but we still managed to have some fun. A couple of nights, I went with a few of my teammates down to the main Athletes' Village in Bride-les-Bains to visit. We wound up getting trapped down there because the gondola shut down and we couldn't get back up. We had to take the gondola in the morning and scoot to practice.

Our head coach, Dave King, certainly made sure we were in top physical shape entering the Olympics. Sometimes I thought he must be crazy because of all the things he put us through. We'd practice early in the morning for at least two hours, and then we would hop on the exercise bikes or do weights. I was lucky I'd lived with Burkie in Calgary. He kept me going through those early-morning practices. He would keep saying, "Just do it. This is the way it is. Don't worry about it."

It was also hard playing all those exhibition games we had against the U.S. They were nothing games, and they seemed endless. Dave kept saying, "We're building towards something," but I had a hard time believing that at the time. Once we got to Davos, Switzerland, for our final training camp, though, I really picked up my game, and I was ready.

Off the ice, my relationship with Dave was a bit jagged at times. But inside, I knew what he was doing and he knew what I was doing. I respected him, and I think he respected me, so we just went about our business. Dave King is an excellent person at heart. He was always there for me. When a couple of Quebec MPs tried to get me kicked off the Canadian Olympic team because I refused to sign with the Nordiques, he stood up for me.

We started the tournament with a game against the French—the host team—on the same day as the opening ceremonies. Although we were heavy favorites, we were scared and nervous before the game. They had everything to gain and nothing to lose, because no one expected them to win. That's when a team can be really dangerous. Meanwhile, we were tight. Everybody was jittery. They gave us a tough game, but we were able to come away with a 3-2 win, thanks to some great goalkeeping by Burkie—and that's all that mattered.

We had a police escort straight from our game to the opening ceremonies. It was a thrill to walk into the stadium as a member of the Canadian Olympic team. The blood was pumping. I thought we looked good in our outfits. I was impressed by the innovation of the design. We were the only country whose uniforms showed up at night, because they glowed in the dark. When the lights went out, they knew where Canada was!

We also made sure they knew where Canada was in our next game, against Switzerland. It was time to "put 'er into gear." Dave King had given four of us heck for our performances against the French—me, Joey Juneau, Jason Woolley and Chris Lindberg. He was mad at us for not doing our jobs, for not being the best we could be. He kept it short and sweet. He told me, "You're skiing, not skating." So I picked 'em up. It was time to show the world, "We're Canada and we're boss. It's going to take a lot to take it away from us." We did just that, whipping the Swiss 6-1.

From then on, I think we just took the bull by the horns. We kept the ball rolling with a 10-0 romp against Norway. Then we beat Czechoslovakia 5-1 in a really critical game. Burkie was outstanding once again. Joey Juneau was great to watch, and he scored one amazing goal with a couple of Czech players all over him. Some players who were really struggling at the start got it going that game.

I really didn't feel any pressure during the Olympics. I just felt like a regular player. Dave King and the coaching staff gave me a role to play and I just had to go out there and do my job. My attitude was, "Just do the best you can do." But there certainly seemed to be a lot of media and public pressure on other Canadian athletes. I was really disappointed in the way we treated some of our athletes when they didn't reach the expectations the media had for them. I thought it was unfair. The men's ski team had a rough time. And I felt bad for figure skater Kurt Browning. He had a tough Olympics, but that's no reason to dump all over him. He tried his best. He might have slipped here or there—well, I slip all the time, but I have sixty minutes to prove myself every game.

It was great when Kerrin Lee-Gartner won the gold in the women's downhill. The place went nuts—"Canada won gold!" It was a big relief for all the athletes to know for sure that Canada was bringing home a gold medal. We were staying ten minutes away from the hill where she raced, and some of the guys were in the Village when she won. They told me that it was a blast—that people were running up and down the main street with Canadian flags, yelling and screaming. They'd yell at you if you had your Canadian jacket on and you *weren't* yelling and screaming!

We lost our final round-robin game 5-4 to the Unified Team (formerly the Soviet Union), but still finished ahead of them in first place in our pool. We knew we could hold on to the top spot as long as we didn't lose to the Unified Team by three points or more. We were losing 4-2 but scored twice in the third period to tie it.

I was doing anything I could to rile their bench and give us an edge, and if it meant getting their coach Victor Tikhonov bent out of shape, I was ready to go for it. We exchanged a few greetings after I bodychecked some of his players. The language barrier wasn't a problem in getting our message across.

Good old Victor was quite the master of psychological ploys himself. He'd stare guys down when we were in the cafeteria. He wouldn't sit with his team. He was trying to intimidate players. He'd stare at players on our team, the Swedish team, any team that was around. So I'd just glare right back at him. The old man wanted to win. As a competitor, you always admire somebody who wants to win. I'd just walk past him and say, "Hi, Big Vic."

Finishing first in our pool meant we got to face the Germans in the quarterfinals. It was supposed to be a bonus, since they were considered the weakest team from the other pool. No one would ever have believed what an eventful matchup it would turn out to be.

"This is do-or-die, you know."

I wasn't about to argue with Dave King's assessment of the situation as I took to the ice for the sudden-death shoot-out against the Germans. He summed it up pretty well. You don't get many second chances, so you sure don't want to blow them.

I can't remember how nervous I was, but I know that my heart was pounding at an incredible rate just watching a replay of the shoot-out a month after we got home. It was unbelievable. I thought my heart was going to pop right out of my chest! But as a player, you have to like those situations. It's where you want to be—in the thick of it. You want to come through. I wanted to be there.

I was just thinking, "It's up to you. Be the best you can be. Just put it in the net."

My teammate Wally Schreiber, who had played against the goalie we were facing in the German league, had given me a bit of advice. He said, "Listen, I play against this guy all the time. Just keep it low." But no one can really tell you how to score on a breakaway. It all depends on the situation. I think a goalie has the advantage on breakaways. You can't decide what you're going to do before you go in and shoot. You have to see what the goalie gives you. I thought I'd made the right decision earlier on the first shot, but I'd shot it too high.

Before I took my shot, I went over to Sean Burke for a quick chat. Burkie simply said, "Eric, just put the damn thing in the net."

It was all a blur after that. I skated in, gave the goalie sort of a head fake, went to the right and just fired the puck hard and low. The biscuit was in the basket! Team Canada was up on top!

Just like so many other times in the tournament, we needed Burkie to come through for us again to win the shoot-out.

OTHER VOICES:

Sean Burke

When the German player took that last shot during the shoot-out, I felt the puck hit me really solidly and my first reaction was not to move. I felt pretty sure I had the puck and I had made the save. Things were just kind of frozen in time for a second. The player didn't raise his stick to show he'd scored and the referee didn't wave anything off to show he hadn't, so I just froze for what seemed like a couple of seconds, though it was probably nothing like that long. Then I saw the referee give the signal for no goal.

I got up and turned around to see where the puck was. Part of it was just on the goal-line. I like to say that part of it was just on the line—that it wasn't even close—but I guess in reality it was RIGHT on the line. But that gives you at least an inch, an inch and a half, because the whole puck has to be over the line for a goal.

I didn't see a replay of that until a couple of days later. It was kind of a weird feeling to see how you make a save, and then the puck pops out and drops down. It was like spinning a quarter on a table—it just kind of wobbled and fell flat. That's what the puck looked like. It could have rolled over the line very easily, but it just happened to wobble at the right time and fall flat right on the line.

You couldn't write a better ending. You could make a movie of that whole game and that scene and people would say, "Ah, come on. That couldn't happen. That's ridiculous." But it did.

<hr />

OTHER VOICES:

Dave King

There was no question in my mind when Eric's second opportunity came up that the puck was going in. I had absolutely no doubts. I knew for sure that the Germans would have to score to tie it, because I just knew that he wouldn't miss twice.

I think you recognize one thing right away about Eric—he likes to be playing in big situations, so you're going to put him in there. When you know you're the first shooter in the second round of a sudden-death shoot-out, the heat is on. You want a guy with some poise. Some guys can't handle it, but there are other guys who like it. Eric enjoys that stuff.

The shoot-out captured the imagination of a lot of hockey

fans. What will always make the 1992 Olympic Games memorable was that game. The only questions that I ever get asked are about the shoot-out game against the Germans.

It's nice to be part of an event that makes people really proud to be Canadian. It doesn't happen very often. The attention of the entire country seemed to be on that event. And our guys were in it. And it wasn't the top NHL guys—it was a bunch of kids who worked hard, played well together, really went for it and found themselves on the edge of a dream. I think people really saw effort, and I think that's what people will respect this team for.

We received bags of fan mail the morning of our final game—over 31,000 letters! Schools were writing letters. A nice lady in Trenton, Ontario, sent me a little tie rack with five rings on it to represent the Olympic rings. It's my medal from her. People were writing letters saying, "Gee, I got caught up in it. It made me proud to be a Canadian."

I thought Eric played really well in many aspects of his game during the Olympics. I saw him make great passes. I saw him score some nice goals. He had some devastating bodychecks. He was so disciplined. He didn't take any foolish penalties. He played an accountable game—the consummate team game. That really stuck out in my mind. It wasn't "The Eric Lindros Show." It was, "Hey, I'm playing for Canada. I'm part of it." I think he's a great young guy.

A story came out just as the Olympics started claiming that I wanted to cut Eric from the team. I'd like to know where these kinds of stories come from. This one alleged that Bonnie Lindros and I had had an argument. I hadn't talked to Bonnie for about six months, so it really was a complete surprise to us when we heard about it.

Eric and I both kind of joked about it, and I think it brought us closer together. Something like that makes you realize the importance of communication. You know you've got to work together, because if you don't, people will try to find a way to drive a wedge between you.

———

We came out with a good effort in our next game to beat Czechoslovakia 4-2 in the semifinals. The win set up a gold-medal showdown with our old rivals with the new name, the Unified Team. It's hard to get used to calling them the Unified Team. When it comes to hockey, I think we'll always see it as a Canada-Russia matchup.

We were all business after beating the Czechs. We had guaranteed ourselves at least a silver medal, but the goal was gold. That was something we didn't want to lose sight of. Dave King had borrowed a gold medal from Sylvie Daigle, one of the Canadian short-track speedskaters, and brought it out to show us between the first and second periods. All the guys took a good look at it. It made a big impression. We were thinking, "This is what could be around my neck with forty more minutes of effort."

We almost pulled it off—we were twenty minutes away from winning it all. The score was tied 0-0 after two periods against the Unified Team. Again, Sean Burke was a big force for us in goal. Unfortunately, it just didn't happen. We had some power play opportunities—we came really close—but we couldn't do it. We lost 3-1 to the Unified Team.

Some players were crying in the dressing room afterwards. It felt empty at the end. I was interviewed right after the game and I guess my disappointment was pretty obvious. Some people couldn't understand why I wasn't happy with a silver medal and what we had accomplished. Well, as a competitor, I couldn't feel happy right at that moment. We had won silver two days before with the win over Czechoslovakia. We'd lost gold that day. It was only later that night and the next day that we finally began to feel pride in what we had accomplished—Canada's best Olympic hockey performance in thirty-two years! I was very proud to be a part of it.

Epilogue–June, 1992

Flying High

It took owner Marcel Aubut and the Quebec Nordiques more than a year before finally deciding to trade the rights to Eric Lindros. Then, in a matter of minutes, they managed to trade him twice—to two teams.

In Montreal, on June 20, 1992, the day of the NHL Entry Draft, Aubut made deals with both the Philadelphia Flyers and the New York Rangers for the rights to Lindros. The National Hockey League had to call in arbitrator Larry Bertuzzi, an independent lawyer, to settle the dispute. Bertuzzi listened to five days of evidence from 11 witnesses, including Lindros, before announcing his decision on June 30—ten days after the original trades.

Bertuzzi pointed out that, less than 24 hours before the draft deadline, no fewer than eight clubs were serious contenders in what had been dubbed "the Lindros Sweepstakes." They were all in hot pursuit of his rights.

In addition to the other clubs, Quebec had been negotiating with Philadelphia for some time leading up to the draft. On draft day at 1:00 a.m., Aubut went to Flyers' president Jay Snider with his final position on players, draft picks and cash to be involved in a trade. "This is the deal," Bertuzzi reported Aubut as saying. At 10:30 a.m. that day, Snider called Aubut to accept his terms, a deal that hinged on Lindros agreeing to go to Philadelphia. About 45 minutes later, Aubut gave Snider Eric's phone number, something he had refused to give any team until a deal had been confirmed.

Bertuzzi continued with his description of Aubut's actions. At around 11:30 a.m., Aubut went to the Flyers' room and asked how things were proceeding. Jay Snider gave him the thumbs up. Snider was on the phone at the time with Lindros, who had responded that he had his bags packed, ready for Philly.

At noon, Aubut returned to the Philadelphia room with different news—he had accepted an offer from the New York Rangers. Bertuzzi said that at 11:50 a.m. Aubut and Stanley Jaffe, the corporate operating officer at Paramount Communications, the Rangers' owners, had concluded a deal.

Aubut's wheeling and dealing in the final moments created a fire storm of criticism. The pressure of the intense negotiations had apparently exacted a toll on the Quebec owner. Bertuzzi said many witnesses described Aubut as being "constantly hurried and agitated" in the days leading up to the trade. Aubut himself admitted that things were "pure hell."

Aubut, who had tried to put the heat on the teenaged Lindros throughout the year-long ordeal, now found himself basting in his own cauldron. Edmonton general manager Glen Sather, who has been part of five Stanley Cups with the Oilers, blasted Aubut with both barrels for his handling of the affair. "The Lindros fiasco was created by Marcel Aubut, who has been doing this kind of negotiating for years," Sather told the Edmonton Sun. "It's time somebody stood up to him and told him to stick his negotiating where the sun doesn't shine. It's typical Marcel Aubut. He's trying to orchestrate and squeeze somebody to get another buck. The real crime is, he's going to be a winner any way it works."

Aubut was lambasted from all sides in the media. Toronto columnist Christie Blatchford wrote, "It turns out in the protracted battle of wills between Quebec Nordiques' owner Marcel Aubut and Eric Lindros et famille, the guy who behaved all along like the responsible adult, like the proverbial class act, was the teenager.... It wasn't Lindros who agreed to a deal first with one club, then with another for more dough; it wasn't Lindros who tried to back out of the first deal. It was Bébé Aubut."

In his decision, broadcast live across both Canada and the U.S. on The Sports Network, arbitrator Larry Bertuzzi ruled that Marcel Aubut and the Quebec Nordiques had made an enforceable deal with the Philadelphia Flyers. The Nordiques received forwards Mike Ricci and Peter Forsberg, goaltender Ron Hextall, defencemen Steve Duchesne and Kerry Huffman, a 1993 first-round draft pick, $15 million (U.S.) plus "future considerations," which turned out to be Chris Simon and the Flyers' first-round draft pick in 1994.

Bertuzzi pointed to the facts that Philadelphia had accepted Aubut's terms and that the Nordiques' owner had given the Flyers Lindros's phone number. He said these were clear evidence a trade had been agreed to. "Witnesses from more than one club clearly stated that Aubut would only permit the club to speak with Lindros once it had a deal with Quebec."

For Eric Lindros, the waiting is finally over.

I'm pumped. I'm jacked to the nines. I can't wait to get started with the Flyers. From what I've read, Philadelphia is a town where as long as you work hard and give an honest effort, the fans and organization will respect you. They love people who work hard. I'll make sure I do my best. Things that are great don't happen easily and sometimes it takes a long while to make the best possible match. I honestly feel that's what's happened with me and the Philadelphia Flyers.

I got a phone call telling me it was Philadelphia just before Mr. Bertuzzi went on television to make the official announcement. I listened to how he reached his decision. I think Mr. Bertuzzi made an honest effort. He based his decision on ethics. It's great to finally have my future resolved. Even better, I finally get to wear a baseball cap with the logo of my NHL team on it—my brother Brett and I dashed out to a sporting goods store right away to pick one out.

I'm a little nervous about my first NHL season. I want to go out there and prove myself. But then I try to think about it realistically and view it as being the same thing as junior, only on a bigger pond. I've had to work hard to prove myself at every level and I don't expect it to be any different in the NHL. If you want something bad enough, then you've got to be prepared to make the necessary sacrifices. I know that I will.

I'm not looking for personal goals. If we can improve as a team from the first day of training camp to the last day of the season, everything is going to move forward. As Flyers' owner Ed Snider has said, "Our goal isn't to make the playoffs. Our goal is to win the Stanley Cup." As long as we do things methodically and everyone works together, it will be a great time.

It's all a matter of building. I wouldn't say we're starting from scratch, but we're not exactly front-runners this year. We'll see what happens. If we can improve by 15 points our first season, that's a great start. It's not a matter of me going out and scoring 50 goals or getting 100 points. You can't put a burden like that on yourself. I'm going to do the best job I can and whatever happens, happens. Just as long as the team's winning, the team's moving forward. If you're part of it, that's what's important. They're building a new Spectrum in Philadelphia and hoping for great things. I just hope I can be a part of it.

It's a great organization. Russ Farwell, the general manager, Bob Clarke, the senior vice-president, and team president Jay Snider have really helped me out from day one. The entire staff has made me feel welcome. Bill Barber, who like Mr. Clarke was a star with the team during the glory days of the Flyers and is now the chief of scouting, called me up and offered to help me out any way he could. I've spoken to some of the players. Everyone's ready to go. The coach, Bill Dineen, has told me, "Just go and do your job and everything will work out fine."

I love what I've seen of the city so far. It's not huge but it has a big city attitude. The place where I'm going to live in my first season is just eight minutes from the practice rink and 11 minutes from the Spectrum. It doesn't get much better than that.

The press conference in Philadelphia announcing my signing was a lot of fun. I finally got to pull the sweater of an NHL team over my head. It was a frustrating year but it's over, and it's time to move on to bigger and better things. My parents were with me at the press conference, along with my friends Shannon Finn and Jeff Hardy. My Mom and Dad have done so much for me and have taken a lot of heat for it, undeservedly so. My parents were doing what was right for their kid. I can't understand why people won't accept that. I was 18 years old dealing with big business. I mean, this is BIG TIME business. It isn't nickel and dime stuff. I didn't know how to do it all. I found out that you can't trust anyone more than you can your family. They were all there for me when I needed them—my Mom, my Dad, my brother Brett, my sister Robin. Robin is the youngest, so she was often the easiest target. But she never wavered in supporting her big brother.

Another base of support that really helped throughout the year was letters we received from people across Canada, the U.S. and Europe. It was nice to know that, even though we were often being bashed publicly, an awful lot of people fully supported my stand and took the time to write and tell us.

I just couldn't play for an organization that treats people and does business like the Nordiques. It really bothered me to see the way they treated Mike Ricci, my former world junior teammate and one of the players from Philadelphia involved in the trade. They brought him to Quebec City for a news conference, during which Marcel Aubut said more than once that, in his view, the New York Ranger deal was a better one. He said it right in front of Mike with all the media there. He was putting down Mike and the other players involved in the trade, and I know Mike was hurt by it. I guess the Nordiques haven't learned that players are people, not machines.

I'm often asked if everything I went through with the Nordiques was worth it. The answer to that is an emphatic "Yes!" It was definitely worth it. No doubt about it, I would do it all over again if I had to.

It was a long 15 months, but hopefully I've got 15 great seasons of hockey ahead of me in Philadelphia. It's an amazing feeling. The bird on a wire has finally been set free. Now, all I want to do is play.

ERIC LINDROS

Center **Shoots: Right** **Height: 6′ 5″** **Weight: 232 pounds**

Born: London, Ontario, Feb. 28, 1973
Hometown: Toronto, Ontario

Season	Club	GP	G	A	Pts	PIM
1988-89	St. Michael's Junior B	37	24	43	67	193
1989-90	Detroit Compuware Tier II	14	24	29	53	123
1990	World Junior Championships	7	4	0	4	4
1989-90	Oshawa Generals	25	17	19	36	61
1990	OHL playoffs	17	18	18	36	76
1990	Memorial Cup	4	0	9	9	12
1990-91	Oshawa Generals	57	71	78	149	189
1991	OHL playoffs	16	18	20	38	93
1991	World Junior Championships	7	6	11	17	20
1991	Canada Cup	8	3	3	6	8
1991-92	Oshawa Generals	14	9	22	31	54
1991-92	Olympic Team (exhibition)	24	19	16	35	34
1992	Olympic Games	8	5	6	11	6

Honors and Highlights:

Member of Canada's silver-medal winning team at the 1992 Winter Olympics in Albertville, France—the first medal won by a Canadian team in 24 years and the first silver in 32 years.

- Recipient of the Viscount Alexander Trophy as Canada's Top Junior Male Athlete of the year for 1991.

- At 18 years of age, became the youngest player ever to be named to the Team Canada roster for the 1991 Canada Cup, and was a key member of the gold-medal winning team.

- Selected first overall in the 1991 National Hockey League Entry Draft, June 22, 1991.

- Winner of the Molson/Cooper Canadian Hockey League Player-of-the-Year Award, 1990-91; the Valvoline CHL Top Draft Prospect Award, 1990-91; and the Transamerica Life CHL Plus/Minus Award, 1990-91—only the second player to score a hat trick at the CHL national awards presentation.

- Member of Canada's gold-medal-winning teams at the 1990 and 1991 World Junior Championships—the first time a country has won back-to-back gold medals at that event. Played in a third consecutive World Junior Championship in Germany, 1992.

- Youngest player at the 1990 World Junior Championships. Named most valuable forward and first team all-star center at the 1991 World Junior Championships.

- Member of the Oshawa Generals' Memorial Cup championship team in 1990. Voted all-star team center at Memorial Cup.

- Voted the most valuable player in the playoffs for the St. Michael's Buzzers when they won the Ontario Hockey Association Junior B title in 1989.

• Winner of the *Hockey News* Junior Player-of-the-Year award, 1990-91, and co-winner with Mike Ricci in 1989-90.

• Member of the OHL team in the 1990 and 1991 OHL/QMJHL All-Star Challenge (OHL captain and OHL player-of-the-game in 1991); winner of the Red Tilson Trophy (OHL most valuable player) and the Eddie Powers Memorial Trophy (OHL scoring champion) in 1990-91; set OHL record for most game-winning goals in a season (16) in 1990-91.

Randy Starkman is a journalist who has traveled throughout the world reporting on sports. Currently a sportswriter with *The Toronto Star*, his work has appeared in Canada's major magazines and newspapers, including *Maclean's*, *The Ottawa Citizen*, *The Gazette* in Montreal, *The Globe and Mail* and *The Vancouver Sun*. He is a past winner of the Doug Gilbert Media Award for sportswriting and was nominated in 1990 for a National Newspaper Award. His own hockey career was rather less stellar than that of his co-author; he tended to be the worst player on his house league teams. This is his second book. He lives in Toronto with his wife, journalist Mary Hynes.